I guess that all this is why I wrote the book and continue to welcome opportunities to work with coaches and their teams. It calls on me more to be who and what I want to be than most things that I have done to earn a living in my life. I hope you enjoy the book. As for me I hope to be riding off into the sunset while the townsfolk ask. "Who was that masked man?"

ACKNOWLEDGEMENTS

I want to thank Andrea Gaston and for asking all the right questions and for proving that management and leadership go hand in hand. Thanks also to my lovely wife, Melanie and our cats Emily and Killer for not laughing at me when I said that I was going to write this book. Actually I think the cats did laugh, but how would I know?

About the Author

Don Saracco has been working on individual and organizational performance for more than thirty years. A native of Illinois, he graduated from Southern Illinois University in 1968 with a BS degree in elementary education.

After graduation Don joined the United States Air Force. He served for nearly six years as a commissioned staff officer in the United States and in several foreign countries. He was a distinguished graduate from Officer Training School and was commended for his leadership as the officer in charge of a Strategic Air Command transportation unit. While in the Air Force, he earned a Master of Arts degree in counseling from Ball State University and was selected to work in the Air Force's Social Actions Office where he worked primarily on solving race relations and equal employment opportunity problems. He returned to graduate school twice after leaving the Air Force. His education culminated with an earned doctorate in Educational Psychology with a specialty in Human Performance at Work from the University of Southern California.

Dr. Saracco's career has included staff and executive positions in a variety of business organizations as well as several stints in consulting roles. He has worked with scores of individual managers and coaches as well as with teams and organizations on the goals of improving measurable performance and professional satisfaction.

He is proud to have been associated with the Golf Program at USC where the Women's Team captured the NCAA Division I championship in 2003. Their Head Coach worked very hard over a period of five years to develop that team and used most of the ideas in this book in her team management processes.

Table of Contents

FOREWORD

There is such a thing as not seeing the forest for the trees or being too close to the problem to see the solution. It is this truth from which I derive the moral authority for writing this book. That and my smattering of experience as a coach coupled with my work of several years with college coaches. The point is that I could only write this if I were not a coach of many years or even a devoted fan. If I were either I would have way too many biases and blind spots. I can work with coaches because I don't need them to be like me or like any hero that I have. Actually I don't have any heroes. I think that Sheldon Kopp was right when he said, "If you have a hero, look again, you have just diminished yourself in some way." I find other ways to diminish myself so I have never needed heroes.

I certainly have aspiration models. I grew up with Roy Rogers and Lash Larue and the Durango Kid and Superman (the comic version) and my father and a host of other characters of such perfection that I could not help but want to be like them. I still do. In some ways this book asks you to be like them as well. It may be more about being a positive force in the lives of others than it is about coaching teams, but I make no apology for that. Great coaches have always been about being a positive force in the lives of their players or they were eventually discovered to be not so great.

My work is all about catalyzing the success of other people. A catalyst is something that enables other things to come together in the right way to produce something good. We try to produce success. Success is not necessarily defined as my clients initially define it but in a more ideal way. I don't want to work with people who are not going anywhere or who don't want more than material achievement. I find that most coaches are the kind of people that I like working with. Since only a few make the really big bucks, most aren't in it for the money or the perks. Sometimes they are in it for the opportunity to hang out with really successful people from the booster club. That's okay. Most of those folks are the kind that I like too.

Chapter 1   What's It All About

Who's in Charge Here?

Take a hard look in the mirror. It's you. The bad news is that you are responsible for running the team. The good news is that you are responsible for running the team. That's why they hired you. Why is this good? It is good because you are ultimately the architect of your own success or failure. You get to experience the pride and joy of accomplishment only if you take on the accountability for something of note and get it done. You may not be accountable for every single aspect of team performance and there are occasional acts of God, but you are responsible for creating an environment for success through the factors that you control. You are especially accountable for your:

> Emotional maturity (authenticity and balance)
> Behavior (skills and actions)

I hope that this book helps with the latter and pushes you in the direction of the former.

Success is not random like a game of cow pie bingo. By the way, cow pie bingo is a much underrated sport and I am surprised that ESPN has not recognized it. I understand that coaching it is a moving experience. Okay, I promise no more bad puns.

Anyway, neither is there an exclusive relationship between effort and success. There are too many factors that influence the ultimate outcome. Every success from winning a war to getting promoted involves some amount of luck. Horatio Alger was lucky to be living in the United States of America where his formula for success had fertile ground upon which to grow. Your job is to help luck along by managing the things within your control in the right way. It's probably even necessary to have a spiritual goodness about you. It certainly can't hurt. In the end you have to work at everything that matters and you may be screwed by fate nonetheless.

It is a measure of your maturity that you pick yourself up, dust yourself off and get back in the race (apologies to Frank Sinatra and whoever wrote that song).

As my granddad used to say, you can till the soil and plant the seeds but only God and the Farmer's Almanac know if the crop will come in. Whether or not you can predict the outcome you still have to till the soil and plant the seed. Actually both of my grandfathers were coal miners but coal miners don't say wise things that can be repeated in polite company so I made that part up.

Coaching Is an Honorable Profession?

Okay maybe that shouldn't be a question but we know from our experience in working with intercollegiate coaches that they sometimes have doubts. One of our clients recently went through some problem solving with a player that resulted, in part, in the player gaining a clearer understanding of the Coach's responsibilities. As the breadth and depth of the role began to dawn on her, the player blurted out, "Wow, I don't ever want to have your job."

So this book is about you as Coach or business manager (the two are nearly interchangeable). It touches on players and teams but is about you. Managing well is an inside-out process. It begins within you and derives its power from your strength of character and skills. I don't have much confidence about altering character with a book but we might be able to add to your skills. If you use more effective practices and work at making better decisions for some time, you will get better results even though your character has not changed appreciably.

The total package of accountability for an intercollegiate athletics coach can be daunting. It calls for being a teacher, a travel agent, a mother/father, a trainer, a role model and an all around perfect person. Imagine a life in which every decision you make is subject to review by a 17 to 22 year-old. If that is not a sobering prospect, you probably have not had any interactions with such people.

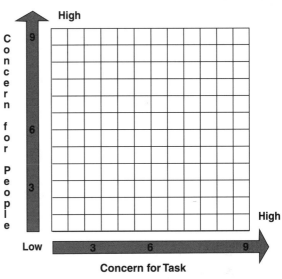

Figure 1
The Managerial Grid

The title of this book comes from what is now part of the mythology of management. Many years ago (during the last century) a team of scholars wrote and taught about something they called the Managerial Grid. A similar model is shown in Figure 1. The authors of this model, Blake and Mouton (everyone in academia is known only by last name) used this model to describe the balanced approach that was the ideal. At the time there was great interest in the world in finding the ideal formula for defining good leadership so that it could be taught to the children of those who owned business organizations.

Pardon the sarcasm. What I really meant to say was everyone knew then as they know now that leadership is very important to the success of collective human efforts such as running a business, winning a war or fielding a winning team. Theirs was a noble pursuit.

You can see that a "9, 9" rating means that the ideal manager or coach has a high concern for task accomplishment and a high concern for people. Essentially he or she is both hard-nosed about things that matter to the bottom line and deeply and sincerely loving toward the people who generate that bottom line. If this sounds like a really good parent or the person that you discovered your drill sergeant to be, you have the picture. It is what a great coach is as well. It is also really, really, hard to find. John Wooden may have been one as well as Ralph Stayer of Johnsonville Sausage fame.

Each has a reputation as a class act who demonstrated deep concern for people while managing a successful (winning) enterprise. A coach recently told us of a recruiting interview in which the prospect said that she was disappointed in her current coach because the coach did not "manage" effectively. Her perception is that a coach is a manager similar to those that we find in the business world. So, stop thinking that you are not a manager. You are.

What Blake and Mouton discovered was that the 9, 9 manager though exceedingly rare, is a good aspiration model for managers in organizations with an authority structure similar to an army or a church. That would be an athletic team. It works for any management role where the leader is expected to be a parent to some extent. That would be you.

Let there be no doubt that your role as a coach is very parental. The team is your "family" in a very real way. The implications of that are very important. It means that getting the best out of your players as individuals and as a team will involve being in their lives in many ways and much of the time. You will have to be curious about their lives in a minimally-intrusive way (they are adolescent after all); help them to think in healthy ways and make good decisions; to handle their emotions well and be respectful of others. You will have to be willing, able and even eager to have fun with them in appropriate ways and you will have to be a model for life for them.

There is no escape from these responsibilities. They may wear you out every day but there is no other reliable path to performance excellence. Coaching is not about you. It is about them. Did you get that?

COACHING IS NOT ABOUT YOU! IT IS ABOUT THEM!

Excellence comes from many things and high on the list of necesary contributions is player-centered coaching. Never forget that. You have a job because there is a game and there are people that like to play it and watch it being played, but most of all you have a job because there are kids who are willing to make the game the most important thing in their lives - at least for a while. They make the game something worth watching by caring deeply about it and by committing a large part of their lives to it. Your job is to respect their commitment by sharing it and by helping them to act on it in healthy and affirmative ways.

I don't know if you wanted a role as parent when you signed up to be a coach. Some people resonate with that part of the role very well. Others do not. If you are comfortable with the general idea of some kind of parenting as part of your job then all we need to do is ensure that you are the best kind possible - a 9, 9 parent. If you don't really like the idea of parenting as part of the job, stop here. Pour yourself about three fingers of your favorite libation, make yourself comfortable and get used to the idea that you are either going to change that feeling or find another career.

There is good news about the role. A parental leader has a great deal of authority to go along with the heavy load of accountability. Your administrative power is almost absolute. What we need to do is ensure that your leadership power is just as awe inspiring. Otherwise you might end up abusing the administrative power and that will serve no one.

The fact is that business organization owners and managers have had to rely on the performance of not-quite-fully-mature people forever and a great deal has been learned about how to get the best from such people. That is to say that a great deal is known about effective parenting though we never call it that in the world of work. The way that I view the relationship between the players on scholarship and the institution is the same as the way that I view employees or associates of any enterprise. They are being paid to perform and performance is defined by the institution and the manager (coach). This gives the coach that load of accountability and authority. This book is intended, in part, to help you to meet the accountability without abusing the authority. It is about the behaviors that are central to being hard-nosed about things that matter and caring deeply for your players.

Just so that I am not completely misunderstood here let me be clear about the fact that not all business organizations need or want parental management. There is a significant segment of the population of workers that want more autonomy and accountability in their work. There are many success stories about organizations that have reached new levels of success by distributing authority and accountability more widely in the organization to enable people to be more quickly responsive to customer needs. These are not college athletic teams though they may be one day.

There will be the occasional player that has enough maturity to be one of those people seeking accountability and authority. Notice I said occasional player. These will be too rare to encourage you to turn over management of the team to the players. When that is done with a group that is not sufficiently mature it is abdication of authority even though it may be dressed up as delegation. This is true whether we are talking about a business manager, a parent or a coach.

I once came into contact with a family where this sort of abdication was going on. The parent, a man in his forties, was addicted to alcohol. Like many who are, he had managed to build many life routines around his addiction so that he could avoid the perception that there was any problem in the drinking. One of his routines involved his walking to his favorite pub in the evening for his daily dosage. This was a good idea because it saved him from drinking while driving. The weird part was that he would have his, at the time, ten year-old daughter drive his car to the pub to bring him home. The man had delegated to his daughter the authority and accountability for ensuring that he got home okay. Do you think this was appropriate? I hope not. It may seem like a bit of a stretch, but I like hyperbole. Sometimes it takes extreme examples to make a point.

An appropriate type of delegation is what you do when you appoint some member(s) of the team as captain(s). Try to remember that ALL delegation represents risk. You are never totally safe when you depend upon others to discharge your responsibilities. Humans are only human after all. Sorry, you still have to do it. It is an integral part of your job of encouraging growth and maturity in the members of your team. The role of team captain must be designed and implemented carefully to minimize your risk and maximize the growth of your players.

Effective delegation calls for clearly defined expectations, legitimate role content and ongoing communication (We might call it performance monitoring, but that sounds a bit harsh.). First, you must make the captain role a real one. The person cannot be expected to be only an extension of you if he or she is also expected to grow. There has to be "weight" in the role in the sense that the person is accountable to you in important ways. It will necessarily become a leadership role so you must define the areas in which you expect the captain to lead. You must also be clear about the areas that are outside the captain's role. For example, captains (like project team leaders) do not make policy or get involved in administrative actions, directly administer punishment or rewards or do anything else that requires "legitimate status and authority." The captain has only your authority upon which to draw and none of his or her own. The captain's ability to lead must be based on earned influence with teammates and not just an invocation of the "god" (that's you).

One of the most important things that team captains do is perform as a "heat sink" or lightning rod for some of the emotional turmoil that commonly besets young people. Players who can clearly see that the captain has your trust and confidence will vent feelings with the captain that are meant for you. It feels safer to do so and they will do so as long as the captain does not rat on them. Captains must be able to sense important issues (a sign of emotional maturity) and bring them to you as issues and not as a surrogate for other players. We have seen players who are very good at using other players as a surrogate in situations where they want to irritate the coach but lack the personal courage to raise issues themselves. One player, for example, who felt that the coach treated another player with favoritism, used other players to raise the issue as if it were a problem for the whole team when in fact it was not. A good captain must be able to filter this stuff while still being a good listener.

In addition to getting good performance good managers have contributed to the positive personal growth and maturation of many young people. In some organizations, such as the military services, personal growth and maturity along with effective performance are explicit goals of the training and leadership processes. Even in some business and public sector organizations it is part of management strategy to foster maturity along with leadership development. It is arguable that neither of these organization types is ever really successful, but I think it is still worth the effort to try. At least it keeps the organization honest in terms of its own character and leadership quality.

There is a great quote in "Harvey Penick's Little Red Book" attributed to his cousin who, when turning over the tennis coaching reins at the University of Texas told the new coach, "Wilmer, I know you'll make better players of your students in four years. But will they be better people? That's the important thing." The deep-in-the-gut real value in excellent coaching is in shaping kids into the kind of people that are good for the world in which they live. I think that winning is the price you pay for the privilege of doing that.

One of our client coaches was faced with a couple of situations that illustrate this part of the role. One player was experiencing one of those common periods of adolescent angst and asked to be released to attend another school where a friend was transferring. The coach's assessment of the situation was that this was most likely a transient episode and that the player would not be better off at the other school. The player was pursuing what we call a geographical cure for psychological pain associated with character growth. The coach's appropriate response was, "I will not let you give up on yourself. You have the ability to be successful here in all the ways that you say you want to be and I will be here to help in any way that I can. Therefore I will not release you." The player got over the angst in a matter of days and went on to be a significant contributor to winning a NCAA championship.

In another case a player committed a serious infraction of the rules. Even though there were some extenuating circumstances, the investigation that followed was an embarrassment to the team and the school. The player wanted to quit the team as atonement. The coach recognized that the best course for the team and for the very quality of the rest of the player's life was for the player to stay on the team. Again, the player recovered and went on to be a real contributor. These are not easy calls to make, but they are your job and you have to think beyond the moment and make decisions that help kids grow as well as perform well.

This book describes how what has been learned about managing team performance in the business world can be applied in the world of sports team management. It is, however, really intended for anyone responsible for leading others. This can be a team of athletes or a business group. While the book is written using a Coach/Player format, I believe that the examples and strategies used are applicable across any endeavor that involves more than one person. So, it turns out that the Grid is a useful framework for us to use in talking about relationship management in any organization where there are owners, managers, coaches or otherwise accountable people who must produce results.

I will provide a framework for developing high performance or more accurately optimal performance in teams. By that I mean that we can only optimize performance within the limits of factors such as the basic talent of each player, the willingness to improve, each players mental disposition, and the dynamics of the team as a whole.   These factors are constantly in flux as goals rise in importance and are discarded or forgotten. As the "Coach" it is your job to **"optimize"** the team's chances for success but you will always have interesting challenges.   There are even different schools of thought about whether or not it is better to have a team with solid talent across the board or a team that depends upon the performance of a couple of stars for its success. The challenges for a Coach are certainly different and different coaches might prefer one or the other type of challenge. I have tried to look at both perspectives but in reality the basic management strategies are the same. It is at the tactical level that the differences emerge.

Will this book help you to make a last place team into a first place team? No, at least not overnight. Teams that are under-performing can and should improve as your ability to lead improves but they are limited by their talent or lack of it. In time and given the addition of better talent on the team, there should be significant improvements in standings, competitive success and overall individual and team achievement. Will the book help you become a better coach? Yes, if you are willing to invest the necessary effort to learn more useful attitudes and behaviors.

One warning before you proceed. I am unabashedly opinionated on subjects that I have strong feelings about so before you read further understand that this is not a research paper for peer review. I have been at this work for a long time and I base what I do on what science tells me. The bad news is that social science is less than exact. This book is about the art of managing performance that has roots in science. If you are looking for absolute truth in social science, fugeddabadit. If you are willing to take on the job with its risks, heavy demands and wonderful rewards, then read on.

Recognizing the Need

Since you are reading this book…or at least browsing through it, I'm going to make a leap of faith that you have already recognized a need in yourself or your team. It may be that you have individual conflicts between players, your team is traveling downhill faster than a first marriage, or you simply want to improve your skills as a coach. One of the principles that we will work from throughout the book is that absolutely no one changes behavior simply because it is a good idea. You have to really get that one because it is pivotal to understanding why some things work and others don't. No one changes behavior just because it is a good idea to do so. There is always something driving that change. Of course the variety of drivers is very large given the diverse complexity of human thinking processes.

For example, witness the millions of people who want and need to lose weight. They talk about it and they make plans to do it. It is, after all, a very good idea to lose weight and everyone knows it. There are lots of "reasons" why one should do it. The problem is that reasons are not motives. The people who are successful at it have some driving force behind their change in behavior such as good evidence that they could die if they don't change or powerful feedback from the environment that matters. The truth is that some do die from obesity and there was apparently nothing in the world that was strong enough to drive them to tackle the problem. The bottom line is that it takes a driver that works for you to get you to change anything. Just because it is a good idea won't cut it. World peace is a good idea - a really good idea, but we don't have it. Golda Meier is quoted as saying that the suicide terrorism would not end until Palestinian mothers loved their children more than they hated Israelis. Makes sense to me.

I hope that what is driving you is something of positive value for you and those whom you would lead or influence. I have seen situations where the drivers are not so positive and can lead a Coach astray. One Coach with whom I worked was initially caught up so much in validating his own past experience that he failed to recognize the need to manage the team from the perspective of contemporary social norms. He wanted the things that worked for his coaches when he was in Little League or Junior Golf or Pop Warner Football to work for him as they had worked with him. Well, times and social models and expectations change. Young people of his generation were less likely to question the absolute authority of the coach, more likely to be punished for their transgressions and certainly lived in a less litigious world. Players and their parents today are as likely to consult lawyers as personal trainers.

If you have not seen a need you might ask yourself these questions:

1. Do you worry that your players don't have enough discipline?

2. Do you struggle with strong players with difficult personalities?

3. Are you facing challenges today that seem overwhelming?

4. Do your players think that you don't give them the support that they need?

5. Are you doing enough to build character in your players along with a great win-loss record?

6. Have you clearly defined your role as Coach?

7. Are you getting all you want from your recruiting strategy?

8. Are you satisfied with yourself as a leader?

If you answered "yes" to the first three or "no" to the last five of these questions you may have a need that you have not clearly recognized. It could also be that you have a friend that is working on some of these challenges. So go ahead. Read the rest of the book. It probably won't hurt and it may help in some direct or indirect way.

So the more compelling the need that you feel the more likely this book will have value for you. Felt need and commitment to change tend to open the mind and heart to opportunities and provide many more "teachable moments" for us all.

Let me be absolutely clear about one other thing. I am not a "sports psychologist" and will not address any of the individual performance issues that a sports psychologist would address. I am fascinated by the dynamics of performance that are impacted by thinking processes, and believe that a good sports psychologist can help boost individual performance on the field. In this book, though, I am deeply interested and involved in the organizational (team) dynamics that impact performance. Frankly any coach that works on only one or the other is missing something very important. While individual performance is crucial to success, it can be cancelled by a rotten team environment and vice-versa.

CHAPTER 2   THE POWER OF COMMITMENT

Goal Setting

Buckaroo Banzai was right. No matter where you go, there you are (rent The Adventures of Buckaroo Banzai for the whole story). That cannot stop you, though, from continuing to go places and the more you are aware and in charge of where you go the better things will be for you and your relationships. A person cannot have any get-up-and-go unless there is somewhere to go. As it turns out people do not just go. They go somewhere. Of course people are sometimes surprised about where they were going when they get there. The answer to the question, "How did I get here?" is usually, "You chose to get here and did the things necessary to make the journey, get over it."

Research over the past twenty years or so has led to a clearer understanding of how human motivation works. Some of what has been demonstrated is that commitment to goals plays an enormous role in generating motivated performance. You can rest assured that all human behavior is goal-directed and that those with the best records of achievement engage in active management of their goal systems. You will want to get this one too. Stop reading now and think about the reality that all human behavior is goal-directed. The implications are critically important. It might be helpful to talk the idea over with a trusted friend just to get clear on where you stand with this. Really getting this may represent a change in your beliefs and such changes do not come easily.

Okay, I assume that you ignored my suggestion and just kept reading so I will go on a bit more about the goal-directed behavior thing. One of your favorite activities is to think about the motives of others. You wonder about motives. You guess about them. You pretend to understand them and are prideful about your special insights where others' motives are concerned. You are fond of saying things like, "Well, she only did that because..." and "That's just his way of ..." and "What the Coach (or boss) wants here is..." The bad news is that sometimes your guesses are really close to the truth. This is bad news because it encourages you to keep guessing and pretending special insight and it keeps you from actually exploring the important information about goals that is the heart of people's motivational systems. In truth you are seldom correct and the more you continue to guess the farther from effective management and leadership you will wander.

Another reason why this is bad news is that your guesses go unchallenged so often that you are encouraged to assume brilliance and insight. After all, there is no readily available information to the contrary. If you look closely you will also notice that speculation about motives is also the stuff that gossip is largely made of. Witness the story that circulated about the sexual orientation of a major league baseball player. The word was that the only reason that he dated women was to hide the fact that he was actually gay.

I hope you know how destructive gossip is to any attempts to build a cohesive team. Gossip and manipulation are two of the enemies of performance that we will face a number of times as you work through this guide. Beware. Players gossip about other players, about coaches and about other teams and schools. Coaches gossip about players, other coaches, about schools, leagues and other teams. And these are only a few of the things that players and coaches gossip about. In truth all relationships are diminished by this sort of guessing and gossip, but I don't expect to change this element in "normal" behavior any more than I expect to discover the secret to cold fusion. It is simply one of the realities that we work with.

You may want to try applying a principle and a technique to help you cut back on your own participation in this destructive process. The principle is one that my mother taught me by example. I can't remember her ever saying anything about it but it was very clear in her behavior. That is that you must always work to ensure that anything you say adds value in some way. This may be a corollary of the "If you can't say something positive, don't say anything at all" rule. The upshot is that you don't start the gossip and rumor process.

Since you cannot avoid being assaulted by gossip from others you should have a way of responding to it that maintains your distance from the process. I like to ask people that share gossip with me what they intend for me to do with the information. Just asking the question tends to make it fairly clear that I don't want to be hearing it and have no intention of passing it on. It is a simple technique but seems to work pretty well for me and for others that have picked it up from me. One thing that it does is help you to avoid becoming the surrogate in someone else's campaign of character assassination.

Okay, on to some "how to" stuff. Managing a goal system is much like managing anything. It helps to think of it as a process that looks generally like this:

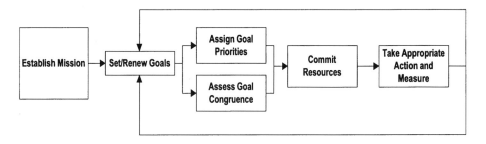

Goal System Management Process
Figure 2

All management flows from a sense of purpose and identity that is usually referred to as a mission by business organizations. Sports teams have a mission as well. I won't pretend to know what that mission is or should be for any given team, but it is crucial that the coach and the team have a sense of what it is. All effective team work is grounded in a clear and understood mission. By the way, I have a personal preference that any mission statement be brief enough so that it can be said in a single breath. Anything longer will neither be remembered nor shared comfortably with others. Here's a possible example:

> *The mission of the Whatsamatta U. Xball team is to*
> *Play well, live right and be winners.*

I know you can do better but I hope you get the idea. Short, sweet and what you want to be and to which you can commit such that it is the foundation for all decisions.

Once a mission is established the team can move on to setting or renewing goals. The overall goal system of the team will consist of goals that are assigned by higher levels of organization management, goals that are chosen by the team for the team, and goals that are held by each individual for themselves. Right away you can see how this system can be complex. At the most basic level goal-setting is about commitment to the pursuit of something of value because a person believes that the pursuit will be fruitful and she or he has positive emotions toward the value and activity. The basic process of goal commitment looks like this:

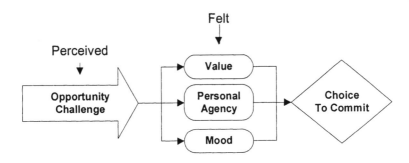

Goal-Setting/Commitment Model
Figure 3

Commitment

When players perceive an opportunity or a challenge they conduct an analysis using several factors that drive the choice to commit.

We recently observed this process at work in a practice session held by one of our client teams. The Coach asked one of the best players to lead a practice drill focused on golf shots from difficult situations such as hitting from the rough and/or around obstacles. The player attempted to demonstrate the different shots but did so in a way that was clearly perceived by the other players as "showing off." Okay, this is your moment for pretending to be amazed that the player would have done that.

The player doing the demonstration had clearly superior skills with these shots than most of the other players but appeared to teammates to have no interest in their learning but only in doing the demonstrations to spotlight exceptional skills. Other players began to walk away and mutter insults. The skilled player's feelings were hurt and the cohesion of the team took a hit.

So, what happened here? The skilled player saw an opportunity to demonstrate skills and to show the other players how these skills add value to performance. All the elements for her to be motivated to do this were in place. It turns out that there was, in the past, an exchange among the players where the skilled player was criticized for being aloof and not socially involved with the team. Her response was that so long as she kept putting strong scores on the leader board, social involvement was not important. Furthermore, she viewed most of the other players as not really mature enough to "hang with" but did not say that to them. She committed to the goal of demonstrating these specialty shots so that she could show them how right her position was. She wanted to make the statement that skill on the course, not social skill is what is important to the team. The demonstration was about her, not about the other players learning something. There was value in showing the shots (prove a point to others and vindicate herself), she knew that she could do it (no question about her personal agency/effectiveness) and she had an appropriate mood (very glad for the opportunity to win a "moral" victory). All the conditions for commitment to the goal were in place - for her. For the other players the commitment situation was a bit more tenuous. They probably saw the value in learning some shots that could make the difference between winning and losing. Golfers usually want to win or at least improve their scores. The value that they place on doing better is one of the critical elements necessary for commitment to a goal.

They probably had some uncertainty about their ability to quickly learn new shots and use them in competition. They had all been playing for a number of years had many coaches helping them to learn the fine points of the game. They knew how difficult it is to learn a new skill and develop it to an expert or competitive level.

By the way, coaches who have a personal history of athletic accomplishment may be tempted to do the same thing that this skilled player did. We know of one coach that spent several years intimidating players with skilled demonstrations without knowing that it discouraged players. Some structured feedback helped the coach to change that behavior so that players could grow with more realistic improvement goals.

The mood support of the players in our example may have been a little weak as well since there was some lingering dislike for the skilled player. Their commitment was at best soft and at worst completely lacking since they abandoned the activity at the first sign of apparent arrogance from their teammate.

Here is what happened. The other players were willing to begin the activity with the weakest form of commitment in place - they were willing to show up. What we know is that real commitment is solidified after the first steps toward the goal are taken and initial fantasies about how things are going to come out are fulfilled. If the first steps put you in the dung pile rather than the glow of success, commitment vanishes and motivation goes along with it. That is when the blaming and excuses begin. The other players could have ignored the apparent arrogance of the skilled player and worked to learn something of value regardless of the source. They could have. But they didn't. Value alone doesn't have the power to sustain commitment. There also have to be appropriate confidence and a supportive mood.

I suppose that there are some situations where a strong enough value can be enough to overcome shortfall in the other areas, but that kind of value is really rare in life and maintaining commitment in such a situation means real effort must be expended. The whole thing is a very personal cost benefit analysis process that determines how people choose goals.

So, what's a coach to do? My best idea is that if the coach were present in this situation, he or she could have modeled mature learner behavior by asking questions related to the skills being demonstrated. The coach could also have asked other players to try one of the shots and lead a feedback discussion that included feedback for both the skilled player and the others that attempted the shot. No guarantees here, but coaches have to model the right stuff even when it has little apparent effect
in the moment.

Priorities

The next steps in the process, assigning priorities and assessing congruence must occur simultaneously and repeatedly.
Priorities are necessary to help with decision-making. They tell the coach and the team what is most important. A major problem with

prioritizing goals is the tendency to create "horizontal priority lists." Many managers and Coaches will avoid discussion of priorities for fear that people will let some important things slide. That kind of thinking can easily come from not understanding that goal systems must be managed dynamically.

Some folks seem to think that goals have to have a kind of absolute permanence - that once set a goal cannot be altered. That is almost true for strategic goals. They require a degree of durability because large scale achievement tends to involve more resources and longer time frames. Thus strategic goals put more at risk and call for more certain commitment. The commitment also requires very frequent renewal as is the case with all goals.

There may be some goals that are always at the top of the heap -- such as winning. That's really what Vince Lombardi was getting at when he is quoted as saying, "Winning isn't everything, it's the only thing." For him no matter what else happened to be true winning was still the top priority. Some business organizations operate with goals like customer satisfaction as always in the top slot. Ford Motor Company built an advertising campaign around quality being "Job 1." This was a clear statement that everyone's top priority at Ford was quality regardless of the situation. Let's all say, "Thank you very much" to W. Edwards Deming and our Japanese friends for this emphasis on quality. Supposedly no other goal at Ford could supercede quality though I will bet that safety would not be ignored in order to meet a time commitment. At least I hope so for the sake of Ford's employees. Priorities take constant affirmation and renewal since changes in situations will change the relative importance of things.

I heard a comment from a successful football coach the other day that seems to capture something important. He said that his team worked constantly on being winners, not on winning games. He did not elaborate but it was easy to get what he was saying. Winners tend to win games and become champions. Those who concern themselves only with winning games will be open to bad strategy choices and can end up being losers even when they win.

I have always wondered, by the way, what happens to those movie heroes who knock the guy off the motorcycle or bicycle, take the vehicle and chase the bad guy which to him and to us in the audience looks like a very important goal. More often than not the cycle ends up destroyed in some way. Do they get sued or have to face criminal assault charges after the honeymoon with the beautiful co-star? What about the guy who got knocked off his bike on his way to the most important interview of his career for which he is now late which leads him to commit suicide in a fit of deep depression?

I went too far there didn't I? Sorry.

Anyway, the point is that priorities are necessary to enable decisions but must not be used to defend failure to get things done. The truth is that we are all expected to exercise some judgment day to day and moment to moment because sometimes the relative priority of goals is situational. For example, the priority for a given practice session may be work on a specific aspect of the game where the team has shown weakness in recent competitions. That does not mean that other aspects of the game are not important. The next practice session may need to focus on another goal or set of goals entirely. What was of paramount importance yesterday is secondary today. That is the nature of goal systems and one of the reasons why they must be actively managed.

The type of goal can also be important if you are helping your players to set personal goals. In the view of many experts (and me as well) performance goals have more positive impact than outcome goals. The difference is usually described in terms of individual player control. Whereas outcome goals such as winning a championship or leading a league in some statistic are not completely within player control, goals that point to improvements over previous performance such as more first serves in or more fairways hit are completely within player control. You will still read about successful coaches and players who have outcome goals. They must not have read the research. By the way, the least useful goals are "do your best" goals. These seem to have almost no impact on performance at all. So, while winning the championship is an important strategic outcome goal, I cannot work on it in practice. I can work on my swing or my footwork or my knowledge of the playbook. Those are within my control and if I and all of my teammates do better at the fundamentals we will be more likely to have a shot at the championship.

Teams too may do better with performance goals. It should be better to set a goal such as "improve the team score by X points or strokes or whatever" than it is to set a goal to win a particular game or tournament. The tournament wins and league standing improvements will come as a natural outcome of performance improvements - especially if the other teams cooperate and do nothing extraordinary.

Congruence/Compatibility

Congruence, compatibility and priorities are closely linked. Congruence simply means that there is no important conflict between and among goals - they are compatible. I am reminded of one player that spoke freely of the need for determination, hard work and commitment as necessary for great performance. It was great to hear her speak of how important it is to give one hundred percent to preparation and practice and to have clear focus during play. Then in the next breath she would qualify all of that fine championship rhetoric by saying that she also needed to have "fun" in her life. Fun translated into practicing less during the off-season. She claimed that the tension and stress of such dedication and focus needed to be relieved by ensuring that she had enough fun. She often used this need as a reason for failing to spend time and effort on the practice that she asserted was crucial to success. Go figure. I guess people get confused sometimes. I think that they also learn the language that tells others about their commitment to the game and they say the right words at all the right times as part of a personal PR strategy but have competing goals in their personal system.

Coaches can easily go bananas trying to make sense of this sort of apparent goal conflict. The key to successful coaching is to recognize that this is a problem for the player to solve - not the Coach. There will be more about problem ownership later. The Coach must focus her or his efforts on helping players to explore and clarify their personal goal systems as well as how the personal system is at odds or congruent with the team's goal system. There is some really good research that makes it clear that assigned goals will produce better performance than self-set goals in many situations. In other situations self-set goals will work better so long as they are congruent with team, group or organizational goals. Self-set goals for performance improvement are the most likely to contribute to both individual and team success. It is good to remember, though, that performance means as a person as well as a player.

What we have in the example of the specialty shot demonstration is, among other things, a failure to have congruent goals among all the participants. The coach wanted to improve overall performance. The skilled player wanted to make a point and the other players wanted to learn without cost to them. While there are occasions where pure congruence is not necessary it sure does help that people are clear about each other's goals for those situations to work. Perhaps compatibility is a better term than congruence since differing goals can be compatible just as different people can be compatible. It is not always about being the same. Many times it is about not being different in ways that interfere with cooperation.

I think that all of the goals in this situation/example can be compatible if every party possesses sufficient maturity. Maturity can act as a "filter" or "moderating influence" that helps people to see ways in which the goals can be congruent.

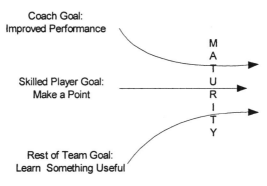

Goal Congruence and Maturity
Figure 4

One of the things that mature people do is find the proverbial lemonade in a gift of lemons. We all hate to see an arrogant person showing off. It takes a very mature person to maintain comitment to learning goals in such a situation. Team leaders are wise to place high value on this aspect of maturity in the players that they choose for their teams and in the lessons that they teach in their work with young people.

I think that the extent to which athletes must be at once self-motivated and relatively immature puts them somewhere in between the extremes of dependence and independence. People in team situations are interdependent. Their initial and most abiding connection is at the level of mission and goals. Shared identity and shared direction set the stage for cooperative action. Everything else is details. Never forget though that the devil is in the details.

CHAPTER 3   A STAKE IN THE GROUND

All movement starts from somewhere. In addition to where the team is going, a coach has to know where the team is. A coach also has to know where he or she is. If you don't know where you are starting from you cannot create a path to anywhere because everything exists in relation to everything else in the "big system." You can be assured that growth and development are necessary and possible. It is a rule of the universe as we know it that you cannot stand still and live. Inaction produces atrophy. That's not acceptable for anyone but catatonics and those who have given up on life. So, some kind of assessment is necessary and useful. The results of assessment then work hand in hand with the "infrastructure" that the coach has built to form the basis for coaching strategies and tactics.

For most teams in both sports and business multiple factors need to be assessed to understand the whole picture. It is not easy. Things continually change, each sport has unique skill components and each business team lives within a unique culture. To keep it simple I will limit my suggestions about assessment to categories that can generally apply anywhere that performance is important.

Coach Skills

There is one question that is the true acid test for whether or not a leader is actually a leader and that is, "Is anyone following?" We use several methods to answer the question ranging from direct observation to structured feedback. Every method works to some extent but structured feedback provides the most valid and reliable information. This is true for a couple of reasons. First, it is based on a complete competency model. That is, it actually provides information about things that make a difference. Second, it filters out the single cases of opinion that can color a picture either positively or negatively. The information is representative of the combined opinions of all stakeholders, not one or two with strong feelings or an exceptional willingness to share their views. Third, it provides complete anonymity of the respondents so there is no chance of retribution. This is really important. One client of ours recently received the news that a judgment had been rendered against them in the case of employees that had provided feedback without anonymity and been fired shortly thereafter. They are no longer using open-ended questions to gather feedback.

Another good thing about structured feedback is that it points us in the direction of why people may not be following as well as telling us whether or not they are. For sports teams we use a tool that we adapted from one that has seen many years of service in gathering feedback for business managers. It is based on a management competency model that is results-focused and recognizes the importance of interpersonal relationships. It is a pretty good measure of nine, nine coaching - or the lack of it. It really gives the coach a good foundation for dialogue with players about expectations and performance as well as a roadmap for changes in management practices.

Player Skills

Assessment of player game skills is entirely your province. I make no suggestion that can help with that.

This is also true for employee technical skills. I assume that coaches have effective ways of assessing game skills even though I know that those ways will sometimes include purely "gut" feel about players. That's fine. We all have a "Bozo Meter" of some sort that registers warning in the presence of people who are "wrong." But don't make the mistake of thinking that you don't need some metrics to make an assessment more than a guess. The science of statistical analysis is really coming into its own these days. Frankly it makes my head hurt, but I understand its importance. We need to have ways to getting validation for our gut feelings or for questioning them. The numbers can do that. You want and need competent players so you have to be able to assess skills objectively while you assess people subjectively for purposes of both recruiting and player development.

And, above all remember that *TALENT ALONE CAN MAKE YOU A CONTENDER, BUT IT WILL NOT MAKE YOU A CHAMPION.* Individual maturity/character and team cohesion are necessary to bring the trophies home.

While I have nothing to offer in terms of how to assess game skills I can offer some suggestions for how you communicate about that assessment. For example, it does little good to spot the one thing that, if changed, can turn an average player into a star if you cannot communicate about it. I will cover that in the chapter on power and accountability since communication is really about power. What, you don't agree? That's okay. Not many people think about it quite that way but it may help if you do.

One thing you must be able to assess is player maturity and specifically emotional maturity. Getting a good read on this can save you immeasurable time and energy because it will be the single greatest cause of problems between you and the player and between the player and the rest of the team. I have alluded to the importance of maturity in a captain. Look for it or for a demonstrated willingness to develop it in all your players. It can help build high performing teams and make your life quite a bit more sane and reasonable.

First, your recruiting has to effectively explore the player's history with regard to emotional intelligence. The best way to do this is to explore with a candidate some personal history with relationships or situations where emotions were involved. There is some specific information about effective interviewing techniques in the section on relationship skills below. The essence of the thing is to find out what strategies the player has used in the past to manage in the domain of emotions. Those are the strategies that he or she will use in the future. They may also be the things that you will have to help the player to unlearn if you decide that access to his or her game skills is so important that you are willing to take on the job of character re-building.

You must also learn to deal with "player drama" in an effective fashion. Drama can kill you and the team if left out of control. Drama is a function of the individual and collective emotional maturity of your players. There is an inverse relationship between these variables. The more mature the less drama and vice versa. I'll bet you saw that one coming.

Of course, you may be one of those coaches that thrive on the drama because you are a drama king or queen in your own right. If you find yourself constantly having to sort out some problem around which there is a great deal of story to be told by everyone involved, then you had better get someone that you trust to give you an informed objective opinion about your status as drama royalty. It could be that you are encouraging drama because you love dealing with it. I have worked with a number of managers over the years that kept coming to me with the same sort of problems in their organizations. After the second or third one of these it becomes clear that the manager is actually encouraging the problem to occur.

A case in point was an executive in a consumer products company who kept having problems with subordinates who could not get along with one another. The faces and names of the subordinates would change from situation to situation but the dynamic remained the same. It turned out that the executive was creating these problems by encouraging the subordinates to paint themselves as victims of each other's bad behavior. All these victims of course needed rescuing and the executive loved to rescue. I got to be the gunslinger from out of town that the heroic executive brought in to help. Solving the immediate problems was not as hard as it was to change the behavior of the executive. Prevention is more powerful but it costs more in the short run.

So assessment with regard to emotional maturity includes self-assessment for you. No team can or will have much maturity where the coach has the same or greater needs for character development that the players have. Anyway let's get to recruiting for good relationships as well as for good player skills. It is always better to design a solid structure than to have to retrofit after each minor earthquake (California wisdom).

Relationship Skills

One of the really fun parts of your job is being the mediator or arbitrator in interpersonal conflicts between players. When you recruit you are going to try to get the best players that you can so that your team is as talent-rich as it can be. Alas the path to greatness is littered with land mines.  Sometimes when you recruit for ability to play the game you will end up with a great player that has the interpersonal skills of a wounded grizzly bear. You could also get a great player with great skills that tend to be used to manipulate rather than to develop healthy relationships.

In some teams that we have worked with there are strong players who come from different countries with different customs and values. Can you spell cultural and language differences? In either case the net effect can be communication problems and conflicts that seem to come from nowhere like a cruise missile.

In the case of the star who seems to rub everybody the wrong way you can take preventive steps or you can commit to the repair work that will become necessary from time to time. The preventive steps may include making the decision that the team is about more than having a star player and not recruiting such a kid. Maybe it is in how you contract with the player and clarify your expectations and the consequences that can be expected. I tend to think that the preventive work is more effective, but some people like the repair work. Maybe it makes them feel good to deal with difficult people and problems. Go figure.

You may also run across a star player who is loved by nearly everyone, but who does things that undermine your authority or are simply destructive in a mischievous way. This one can be way more difficult to deal with. In the first place you may see no evidence whatsoever during your pre-signing investigation process. After all, there will be few people who will say anything bad about the kid. Their coach may have some suspicions but will probably be reluctant to say anything without concrete information that is hard to come by. We worked with one team where one of the better players was like this. He was liked by everyone. Even the players who did not particularly like him could not find anything to say against him. He was funny and friendly and the consummate social organizer. He was the enforcer of time discipline for the team and almost always did a good job when performance counted. The only problem was that he used his ability to attract people in ways that were ultimately not good for the team. He used younger players to provoke arguments with the Coach about rules that he did not like. He used them as his surrogate to lodge complaints about the behavior of other players. In essence he was really likable but lacked the courage to speak for himself and take the risk that he might not be liked quite so well.

The good coaches I have seen will always involve recruits with current team members in social situations that are as relaxed as possible. They observe the way that the recruit and the current players interact and assess the apparent compatibility of the kids. I have no definitive evidence that this works but I can see no reason why it shouldn't help. I think that you must talk with the current players about how they "feel" about the recruit. Not to do so is likely to be viewed as an abuse of your authority. I caution you, though, to not rely too heavily on current players to be a good judge of the relationships that can be developed. There are good reasons why their initial assessment is suspect.

One of the reasons is that teams that have developed a culture and adequately defined roles within it are reluctant to freely accept outsiders even when accepting them can be good for the team and contribute to team and individual goals. That's part of the good news and bad news about teams. We know that teamwork is a phenomenon that exists in nature and appears to have contributed to the success of our species. Teamwork among individuals is a natural, observable and desirable thing under the right conditions. The bad news is that everything must and does change. Teams must acquire new members. Everyone knows that. That doesn't make it easy. Every change threatens the team's cohesion.

The upshot of all this is that you have to realize that even though your current players understand the inevitability of new members joining the team, they may unconsciously resist them. All of the interactions in your unstructured social situations are charged with feelings on both the part of the insiders and the outsider. You will hope for instant affection and rapport because that's the most comfortable way it can go. You may dread the outright rejection of a really good player because you have already committed to that player in your heart. You may get better information from the "social interaction" assessment method if you make it a little more formal.

Consider developing a post-visit reporting format that you require players to complete after having spent time with the candidate. Ask for written assessments of the candidate's fit with the team based on some specific questions. Here are a few examples aimed at getting some thoughtful feedback.

"Describe some specific behavior that you observed during the visit that leads you to believe that this player will be a good fit with the team. Describe at least two or three things that he or she did or said and tell me why you think each indicates a good fit."

or

"Describe some specific behavior that you observed during the visit that leads you to believe that his player will not be a good fit with the team. Describe at least two or three things that he or she did or said and tell me why you think each indicates a poor fit."

When you get the written responses from your players perform a "sniff test" to sort out the thoughtful responses from the "get-over-it" responses.   For example, I doubt that fashion alone should determine whether or not you extend an offer, but you may get some feedback that the candidate should shop somewhere besides the local thrift store.   That is a get-over-it response.   Players must be clean, well-groomed and dressed appropriately, in my opinion, but can be just fine in last year's hemline or fabric. I say this knowing full well that I live in a time when fashion dictates that beltlines are well south of the belly button and barely north of the naughty bits. The lingering adolescent parts of my brain can get this, but the parts I think have grown up can't accept it as a good choice for most people. I expect that you are a better judge of appropriate dress than I am. I tend to be rather conventional and conservative when it comes to the behavior of kids upon whom my livelihood depends.

The whole recruiting process for a sports team seems to me to be very much like a typical recruiting "dance" that goes on in the business world. Based on an apparent record of past performance we will meet face to face with the candidate to make an in-person assessment.   In some higher stakes situations we will invite the candidate to a social function to see how he or she does in an unstructured situation. Seems to cover all the bases, right? Wrong. What we have learned is that many people who interview well and who do well when on their best behavior turn out to be the wrong choice for the job. While I don't want to discourage you from using the "unstructured" social situation as a proving ground, I will suggest an enhancement to your interviewing methods that can add some value to the process along with the written reports from current players.

There is a simple technique that has been widely adopted by recruiters that can help to overcome many of the problems with "gut feel" judgments and trying to elicit normal behavior by pretending that the situation is not formal. The proponents call it "behavioral interviewing" and it is based on the idea that the best predictor of future behavior is past behavior. The technique involves delving into the past of the recruit with questions that are designed to uncover warning signals and indicators of skill. If you want to develop really well-honed skills at this type of interviewing you might look up the work of Paul Green. I think that he published some stuff in the early 80's during the last century (I love saying that). He was featured in a training film of that era entitled "More than a Gut Feeling" so you might find something under that title.

Essentially behavioral interviewing is about asking for information rather than speculation or fantasy. Let's say that you are interested in how a recruit is likely to handle being "dissed" by another player. You can ask how he or she would handle a situation where someone said something in public that angered or embarrassed. You can get a pretty good feel from that question how the player wishes that he or she would handle such things. Or you could ask the player to describe a situation where he or she was really angry at another person and then ask how the player dealt with the situation. While it is true that you take the risk of urging the player to lie (another kind of fantasy) you are more likely to get at what the player is really likely to do. People find it more difficult to falsify emotions when they are accessing memory than when they are being creative (hence the method of method acting). If you probe where the picture seems improbable or lacking in detail you will be able to reveal more of the real person and less of the contrived person that so often shows up for interviews.

You can take this to the bank. All of the real people are less than perfect and you are better off getting an imperfect player whose soft spots you know about than a less than a player that looks perfect but is going to surprise you when you really don't want to be surprised.

Gap Analysis

An important key to assessment is that you have an idea what you want before you start assessing. The more you have made your list of wants explicit by writing them down the better. You can pat yourself on the back for your intuition or sense of things but the more you drag the reality of your own perspective out of yourself so that you can see it the better your decisions will be.

The list should begin as a brainstorm. Write down all of the things that make a great player, team member and all around wonderful addition to your life. Hold nothing back. Put it all down and be honest about things like physical attributes and personality. This is not for public consumption so you don't have to be politically correct either. Write your notes on flash paper if you are concerned about your biases being discovered. For an explanation of what flash paper is send an email to mlc@mlc2resq.com or ask someone familiar with illegal bookmaking operations. On second thought just send the email. I don't want to encourage consorting with what my mom would have called a "bad element."

Next, reduce the list to things that your rational mind tells you are the important characteristics and attributes of a desirable player. When you have that list you should identify the means by which you will gather reliable data about that characteristic or attribute. You may get information from talking with other people about the player, from documentation such as arrest records (just kidding) and news reports, from your interviews, from direct observation or from the reports of current players with whom the recruit candidate has interaction.

When you have written down what you want and how you are going to find out about it, proceed to the actual information gathering. When you have all of the information you think you need about the probably actual characteristics and attributes of the recruit compare with what you said you wanted. At this stage the bargaining usually begins. You see it is a sort of probability game without sufficient solid metrics. That's okay. There are ways to turn fuzzy metrics into something that looks and feels better than a guess. Here is an example.

It is normal for stakeholders like coaches to want their decisions to be informed. That is to say that you want to know the extent of your risks in making a choice one way or another. Your problem is essentially the same one that is faced by the young man trying to decide whether or not to ask the object of his desire for a date. What are the chances that she will say yes or no is the question on his mind. Alas we cannot know what her answer will be without asking. Of course we can apply some reasoning to help with the decision. If the young man is a star athlete, attractive by community standards, and generally popular he can have a fairly high level of confidence that she will agree to go out with him. If, however, our smitten subject is the secretary of the AV Club and has yet to have his first date, we can say that the chances of an affirmative reply would be somewhat less. In either case confidence in our prediction is based on knowing some things and making an educated guess.

We cannot calculate the probability of her answer any more than we can calculate the probability of workplace violence happening in the headquarters of ABC Corp. We can make it look like a calculated assessment by assigning values to factors such as athleticism, relative popularity and dating history, but by doing so I have still only assigned numbers to constructs which are not absolute values (see Figure 5).

The validity of these numbers is entirely dependent upon the quality and amount of real data that I have. I can increase the validity of the numbers by having facts such as the actual number of athletic, popular, attractive boys whose requests for a date have been answered in the affirmative by this girl and/other girls exactly like her. But I don't have that data. What I rely on is my own judgment about what that experience is likely to have been. Even if I had that data I would be missing a great deal of relevant information about the variables that affect girls' decisions when asked for a date. More judgment -- and judgment is not probability -- it is judgment. You may call it "felt probability" if you like but it is still judgment.

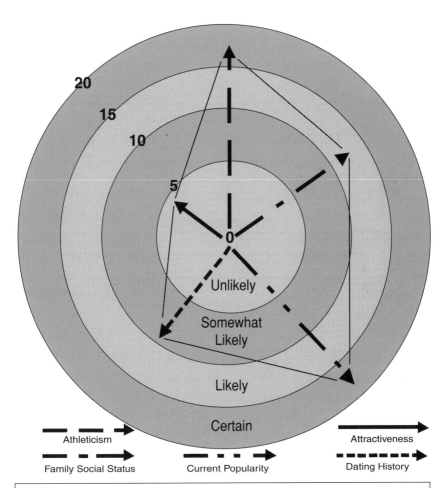

We "rate" the "candidate" on each of these five criteria to get a probability of an affirmative response. Since our ratings reach into or beyond the "Likely" range on three of the five dimensions we think that the data is likely to happen. It ain't science but it works.

To Date or Not to Date
Figure 5

We should not be unfair about the value of informed, educated judgment. The views of experienced coaches are worth a great deal, particularly when that experience can be supported by real data. One area where this is most possible is in the realm of performance measures. Performance lends itself nicely to data

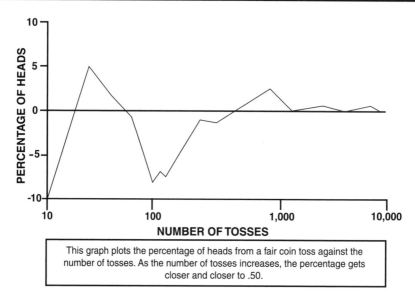

This graph plots the percentage of heads from a fair coin toss against the number of tosses. As the number of tosses increases, the percentage gets closer and closer to .50.

Coin Toss Probability
Figure 6

collection and the creation of data-based history. If a coach has access to performance history data he or she can actually calculate probabilities of future performance with some confidence. Of course those calculations are still dependent upon the volume and types of data. The more data that are available, the more accurate a probability projection will be.

For example, the most well known of probability calculation involves the likelihood of a head or tail appearing after the toss of a coin. We know that there are two possible outcomes so the probability of a given outcome is always 0.5. The truth is that actual probability becomes more and more certain as the number of tosses increases (see Figure 6). You may be able to see that the relative confidence that we can have about data in small amounts must be very low. If a player has competed in a small number of events over some period of time and has consistently produced performance in the top 5% of players at his or her level, we might be tempted to predict similar performance in the future. This is not a compelling amount of data but it is better than nothing and can be used in conjunction with other metrics and your own "feel."

While this sort of thinking sometimes looks a lot like "Kentucky windage" it is the way that most management decisions are made. Management takes place in environments made up of numerous known and unknown variables. It is your job to gather as much science, information and good judgment as you can to support your choices in this often confusing jungle.

You will have made some gut level judgments during the process that are stuck way deep in your psyche (the psyche is located just above the naughty bits and slightly below the belly button). These judgments will enter into negotiations with the reasonable conclusions that you must draw from a comparison of what you wanted and what you appear to have. You will eventually end up somewhere in the gap despite the fact that your gap analysis should tell you that the greater the distance between what you have and what you want the less likely the player should be on your team. In general the most suspect of those gut feelings are the one's in favor of the recruit. They are the ones that make you want to ignore some data that you have.

The feelings that you should pay particularly close attention to are the "warnings" that you get during face-to-face interaction. These are probably based on data you are getting from channels of communication that are not well-controlled such as body language and vocal quality. This stuff is likely to be the most accurate information you get about the person. Pay attention to it.

Infrastructure - The Contract

One of the most important things that you can do as a coach is to recognize that your job is to build a solid and reliable infrastructure around which you and the players can create the details of a viable culture. What's an infrastructure you ask? If we were talking about the nation's telephone system, the infrastructure would be the wires and poles and microwave

CONTRACT
NEGOTIATIONS
UNDER WAY
DON'T DISTURB

transmitters and all the other stuff that provides the essential connections among the many points at which communication originates and terminates. If we were talking about a high-rise building we would be talking about the concrete and steel framework along with the electrical wiring, optical fiber and plumbing around which the building is constructed. These parts of things constructed tend to be durable and fairly permanent.

If we are talking about an organization or team, it is the stuff that, like the steel girders of the building, tends not to change over time. It can be policies and procedures. In business organizations it is often thought of as the information systems hardware/network architecture. It can be the organization of reporting relationships among defined functions. It can be the financial management system. It is the durable practices that make up routines and rituals.

It is also other elements of the culture. For an athletic team it will also be the stuff that tends not to change. Perhaps the most durable thing about a collegiate team will be its institutional traditions. Of course older schools that have achieved more notoriety over time will have the most deeply embedded and well-known traditions even if the recent history of the school is not terribly admirable in terms of win-loss record. Tradition can be powerful and good coaches and good managers alike will leverage it whenever they can. Business organizations such as General Electric, Microsoft and IBM have cultures with the legends, myths and stories that make for strong traditions that help to lift the performance of their people. Any organization that can leverage tradition should do so.

Leveraging tradition can mean using it to support recruiting as well as invoking it as a standard that teams and players must meet. A colleague recently sent me the text of a locker room speech by the coach of a Big Ten school with a long and proud athletic tradition. In the speech the coach exhorted the players to go out and win for themselves, for the team and for the school. He referred to great players of the past as the "ghosts" that would be with them on the field. I don't know if they won the game but it surely demonstrates the point.

So, the infrastructure is the durable stuff -- maybe not as durable as steel girders, but more stable than a teen romance. In a real way it is the stuff of which your "contract" with and among the players is made. Every person in any relationship has a mental model of the contract that is at the heart of their relationships. Some of this stuff is equally well understood by all parties to the deal and some of it is not. A significant amount is understood only by one party and is never made explicit. Making the terms of the contract explicit is what building the infrastructure is all about.

During my time as a marriage counselor, I first discovered the importance of the unspoken expectations, wants and needs that make up crucial parts of the contract. They are the parts most likely to be violated. Marriage partners were very often surprised that their spouse expected things that had never been talked about.

These are things that they would be perfectly willing to do "if only I had known." They included things like calling if you are going to be late and entering any checks you write from our joint account into the register. Not really heavy demands but of sufficient note to push a marriage to the brink of dissolution because any violation may be perceived as a serious one that demonstrates a lack of caring that is unacceptable.

There is plenty of research that demonstrates the impact of contract violation. It results in loss of commitment, feelings of betrayal and emerging intentions to quit the organization (or marriage, as the case may be). We have had a number of calls from worried coaches who have been told by a valuable player about that intention to quit. We have also had calls from players who expressed an intention to go to another school to get away from perceived problems with their coach. These calls can be a symptom of perceived contract breach. Perceived violation often comes in the form of a desire to be released. This is very likely to happen with young college players owing to their relative immaturity and tendency to believe that changing teams will solve whatever problem they think they have with the current team or coach.

The root cause of intention to quit is usually traceable to some perceived violation of an unspoken clause in the contract. The possibilities for perceived violation are nearly infinite. That's the bad news because it means that you will never be able to completely eliminate any chance of their being a perceived violation. Frankly, I think that some of these kids make up clauses for their personal contracts every day. Also remember that they get help with that process from well-meaning others who are fond of telling them what the coach or other players "should" be doing for and with them.

We all want to be liked and personal coaches, parents and family friends are no different in that regard. The bad news is that many people who want to be liked will curry favor by giving unqualified support of the "you can do no wrong" type. This makes the player feel good for a moment and allows them to adopt the status of victim. Victim is a good place for anyone who wants to avoid accountability and we all know what terrible burden accountability can be.

One thing to remember is that you are not the only significant person in the player's life. There are others with whom he or she also has contracts. Some of those contracts are so poorly drawn that they encourage the player to be the worst version of self. The fact that a player has managed to "negotiate" one of those deals will make it a bit more difficult for you to get the deal that is best for you, the player and the team. Don't let that stop you. Just be aware that what seems fair to you may not seem fair to someone who gets a "better" deal from someone else.

By now you have probably realized where this is going. If you want to avoid the perceived violation of the contract you must make it as explicit as you can. It has to be discussed and negotiated and continually revisited as conditions and circumstances change. Revisiting does not mean that it must be changed, though. Again, we are talking about infrastructure and we want that to be durable and consistent over time. Change must not come easily so agreement to clauses in the contract must not be made without sufficient thought about implications.

For example, all of the players with whom we have worked have expected their coaches to "support" them. You may agree that they deserve your support and agree to that being a reasonable expectation with which you are willing to live. Before you agree, however, the question that you must ask is, "What does support mean?" You have to talk about specific examples of support from the player perspective and from your perspective. Agreement must be with a definition that is okay from both points of view. You may not agree that support means you should phone the player every morning to ensure that he or she gets out of bed and goes to class or workouts on time. You may agree, though, that being available on a virtual 24 X 7 schedule if a player needs to talk with you about something important is a part of your job.

I am not suggesting that. It is simply something that seems to be a common expectation. There is a radio sports guy in Los Angeles that does a piece he calls the "Athlete Arrest of the Day" every afternoon. The simple fact that he can do such a spot five days a week raises doubts that I would want to agree to the 24 X 7 calls. The police station to help bail out one of my players is the last place I want to be on Saturday night.

Given all of the above, I suggest that you begin to get clarity about the psychological contract. It is in your best interest to create a climate of clarity around the contract. Every moment of interaction with you and the team, every brochure, every contact with anyone else that may represent the school/organization and every unspoken expectation in the mind of every person involved have impact on the contract.

How do you get that clarity? Through open and honest exchange of wants, needs and desires. The tricky part about such a discussion is that you are the coach and they are the players. Ostensibly you are part of the infrastructure - you will be around longer than they will. You may be fearful of diminishing your authority or freedom of choice by making things more explicit. You may be tempted to define the deal as, "I can do whatever I think is best for the team and you must comply. Furthermore you will assume that everything you do is not only within your authority as Coach but also the right thing to do." Here is a way that you might do this.

Tell each player in your individual planning meeting that you want both of you to look back on your time as members of the same team as a great experience for you both. Tell them that in order to make that happen you want to be sure that you understand one another's expectations. Such a clear understanding will prevent any confusion about direction you might give as well as possible reasons for the player not feeling "supported" by you. Ask them to describe their experiences with past teams in terms of what really worked well and helped them to grow and develop as a player/person. Reciprocate by sharing like experiences of your own. You might disclose some of the ways in which your past coaches met or exceeded your expectations. You can't ask about such things without talking about them yourself first. If you ask without disclosing you will probably scare some kids. You may also want to reassure him or her that your goal is to make sure there are no disappointments, not to pry into things that are past and none of your business. Stay focused on what worked and will work, do not dwell on problems. The problems are all past and there is nothing that can be done about them. You are building a relationship not digging up dirt. Be sure to make clear how you define player and coach accountability to the school, the boosters, to self, and to one another. Accountability differs from expectations in that there may be consequences beyond disappointment for failure to meet accountability. For example, a player that fails to attend workouts or practice or fails to keep up with academic work will be unable to travel, or start or play at all. The phrase that we use in the business world is, "Failure to meet core accountability may result in administrative action up to and including termination." That goes for you as well as for the players, by the way. You serve at the pleasure of the Athletic Director or other executive type and failure on your part has consequences as well. Players need to understand that your behavior sometimes includes balancing your accountability with your deep desire to support the team.

This discussion should allow you to make the definition of your role and your expectations of the player more explicit. It also sets the stage for you having any number of future conversations with the player about expectations and accountability - yours and theirs - that have been met, exceeded or not met at all. If you have not set this structure in place your credibility in talking about expectations met or missed is severely diminished. We can't have that now, can we? If you are at all uncomfortable about this sort of discussion you should find a coach of your own to help you to prepare. Some advance scripting and/or role play should help.

Infrastructure - The Elements

Okay, so the contract lays the basic foundation for your relationship with players. The infrastructure also includes policies, rules, standards, routines, rituals and anything else that needs to remain stable over time to ensure the integrity of the team.

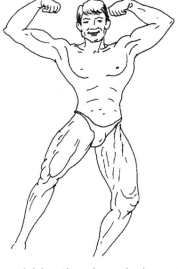

Identity

It starts with things that contribute to the team identity. Tradition is a big part of that for college teams. In business organizations we focus on the "mission" as the primary articulation of identity. In the end it is the "who we are" and "what we do" stuff that everyone understands and embraces. I, of course, like mission and identity descriptions that are simple and easy to understand. A statement of identity or mission should be short enough to say in one breath, have sufficient poetic quality to make it easy to say and be an accurate reflection of reality. Aspiration is in "vision" which is part of the goal system. Identity must be real.

One of my favorites is a statement used by the Ritz-Carlton hotels. It is simple and speaks volumes about identity and commitment to customers. It says, "We are ladies and gentlemen serving ladies and gentlemen." I also liked what we were told about our mission during Air Force Officer Training School (yes, I was a 90-day wonder) years ago. Our purpose was "To fly and to fight." I thought that captured the thing very nicely even though I ended up in charge of people who drove trucks during most of my time in service.

Policies

COMMUNITY VALUES

Policy is organization law. Policy is not created on the fly. It is in place and hardly ever changes. Policy often comes from above. I have often thought that when it does, it should be carved on stone tablets just for effect. I once worked under a commanding general in the Air Force who would issue commands by sending notes on small pieces of personal stationery. These missives came to be called "snowflakes" by those upon whom they fell because they came from the heavens. It was a very real part of our culture in that command. We all joked about it but never failed to take the notes seriously.

Anyway, policy is the law that does not change. You can have policies about anything that is important to the integrity of the team. In my opinion this is your realm. You can and should involve the team in setting and clarifying standards and rules, but policy is your job. There is one very important principle for you to follow. Keep it very, very, very simple. Please don't follow the example of most governments and attempt to manage behavior by legislation. One of the worst things that you can do as a manager or coach is to implement a policy change based on the behavior of a single player. Never make a rule for a person. For a person you make a judgment, not a policy. I am a bit extreme in this belief, but I believe that rule by law is incredibly important to civilization up to a point. At some point (probably where you start thinking about an internal revenue system) law has ceased to serve civilization and begins to destroy it. Here are some sample policy statements for your consideration:

> "We will be a team that believes every player has the potential to be a champion."

> "We will be a team where practice and competitive play are taken seriously."

> "We will be a team where every member seeks and uses feedback on performance (Yes, Coach too)."

> "We will be a team that regularly examines its methods and plans in order to find ways to play better, live well, and compete effectively."

> "We will be a team where mutual respect and support are practiced daily."

I will readily admit that these policy statements may describe the spirit of the law more than the letter of it. Sorry, you will just have to work with me on this. In my opinion policy is about creating the spirit and we rely on your personal character and moral compass to guide the letter and application of the law.

Find a quiet moment and make a list of the "laws" that govern you and your team. Make this a brainstorm - no thought is excluded. When you have your list, refine it by eliminating duplication or identifying the root law that may drive some of the others. Keep narrowing the list to those that really impact the team until you have as few as possible. These are the ones that you want to communicate to and discuss the importance of with your players.

Structure

The structure of an organization defines reporting relationships (accountability among persons and/or functions), authority levels and political systems. The structures of business organizations are often quite complex (such as in true matrix organizations) and do change. When I was in the HR department of a Fortune 500 company many years ago we used to meet regularly to look for ways to restructure the organization in order to afford some talented person a development opportunity or solve a problem of workflow. Structure has become less permanent as the pace and nature of business has changed in recent decades.

Your structure should be fairly simple. It all depends upon the size of your team. Football teams will have larger structures than tennis teams. Teams that bring in lots of revenue can have larger structures than teams that do not. Cherchez le cash is the operative principle.

Your structure usually consists of you at the top, your assistant coaches (paid and volunteer) below you and the player leaders (captains if you have them) below them. The rank and file players are at the bottom. Some people don't like the bottom because there is not much authority there. The good news is that there is much less accountability as well. Your choices about who fills those middle management roles (assistant and captain) should involve capacity to accept accountability. For example, it is my opinion that you are better off having no captains rather than captains that are not up to the job. Please understand that by "up to the job" I mean able to either do the job or grow into it. Both things call for sufficient character development. Remember that a vertical organization takes leaders who are capable of command-style leadership. They are models of behavior and values, they are able to ask others to do things that must be done and they deeply care for the people under them. They are also able to walk that perilous line between the interests of the various members of the team and those of the overall team.

One principle to remember here is that any middle management job has to be real in order to be valuable to you. If you have no intention of authorizing such positions, i.e., empowering them, then don't have them. If they are only window dressing, they are likely to undermine the team. You have enough to deal with. You don't need people in middle management working against you as well. Team captains, for example, are field leaders. They can have a special credibility with players owing to age proximity and greater value agreement (they might actually like hip hop music). They must be more than enforcers of rules. Their role should include substantive leadership. They should be responsible for things like first level conflict resolution and serving as a "fair witness" in problem-solving between players and the coach. These are also things that assistant and volunteer coaches can help with.

Assistants and volunteers can provide support for you and the team in a number of ways. Again, they can perhaps help most by serving as a heat sink to draw off excessive emotions so that players can communicate with you more effectively. They may well have time to listen when you must take care of other team business. They may be able to serve as an example of and coach for character development. They can also be a pain in the gluteus maximus if they do not have sufficient character of their own. They can become part of the drama when drama is the last thing that will be helpful. Choose them with the same care that you choose players and captains.

Make no mistake about it, (thank you, Richard Nixon, for that phrase) team captains can be a powerful positive force on the team but they are not extensions of you. They are part of the management team and they have to earn their role as leader just as you do. Just because you assign the role does not mean that they will be anything more than a joke to the players. When choosing captains and assistants, try to leverage any legitimate respect that the rank and file players have for someone. It can help set the stage for their success and give you more time and energy to devote to strategy and long-term planning. Be careful, though, of willingness to follow what looks like respect but is only misguided hero worship. Kids with less character development can be strongly attracted to older kids with equally little character development who are "cool" for some reason. Choose the player with character over the player with followers and less character. The followers will come and even if they don't you have not put a potential adversary of yours in a position of authority.

Standards and Rules

After you get clear on policy and structure you should move on to standards and rules, which are a little more flexible in the way that a technology infrastructure is flexible because of its need to change over time. Standards are often reflected in the identity. Rutgers University, for example, traces its roots to its founding before the revolutionary war. In its "vision statement" it describes itself as "dedicated to a standard of quality that makes Rutgers a preferred choice for students." Other schools focus on the academic areas in which they specialize or on the research that they do or the number of U.S. presidents that they have graduated. Each statement of identity implies a standard of performance for the school.

Your team will be well served if it also has a set of standards that are rooted in tradition. Like the U.S. Marine Corps which never leaves anyone behind, your team should have some standards of behavior and performance that become part of the identity. These implicit standards are a great foundation for the more concrete standards that you should publish and communicate as part of your team infrastructure. One team with which we have worked has a practice of each player inserting nails into a piece of ribbon and hanging these in the dugout during practice and games. Each nail represents an accomplishment against team and individual goals. I like this as a way of making measurement visible because measurement makes standards real and gives them power.

You may have picked up on the fact that I am a great fan of standards and tradition. I am - unless they get in the way of getting the job done. When it comes to standards and rules I also want there to be as few as possible so that you do not rob the team of necessary flexibility. You should establish both quantitative and qualitative standards because both are necessary to cover the things that are important to the team. The qualitative standards may be communicated as expectations and will usually require clarifying discussion described above if you intend to ever invoke them.

Quantifiable standards include things like attendance (number of absences allowed before a player is benched or taken off the traveling team), lateness (on time to practice, meetings, etc.), repetitions of practice elements over a period of time, participation (in recruiting process or booster-sponsored events), academic standards and dress and appearance standards.

Qualitative standards include things less measurable. They are the "I'll know it when I see it" things like positive attitude and support for other players. If you have standards like these then you must take the time with the team to develop behavioral examples of these things. Examples provide some common ground for understanding what it means to say that a player has a good attitude or work ethic. They are not, however, absolute. There can be behaviors that you did not anticipate which clearly, to someone, demonstrate attitude. A player on one team that I know would sit aside from other players between practice activities. This self-isolation may have been nothing more than extreme introversion or shyness but it was perceived by the coach and other players as an attitude problem that violated their standard of positive mutual support.

I like the idea of the coach developing standards, establishing rules and clarifying expectations with the players. Most of this can and should be done with the team all together. A few things like specific expectations that you have of individual players should be discussed privately. It is worth the time at the beginning of each school year or sport cycle to spend a few hours on this. It is more critical for those sports where individual performance is central such as tennis and golf. The extent to which players in these sports see themselves as independent performers means that you will have to work a bit at establishing an agreed upon infrastructure in order to build any team cohesion. As always, though, the coach must be the voice of reason and have the last word about what will be kept as a standard.   Players may not like even reasonable dress and appearance standards, but if the coach believes that they will contribute to the team image as a winner then that is his or her choice to make.

Of course, most schools today have a "code of conduct or behavior standards as well. Most of these are very much a warning against unacceptable behavior. There is no reason to duplicate these in the team standards, but it might be helpful to review them with players periodically and as part of your beginning of the year standard-setting. This is especially necessary if they are viewed as policy by the institution.

Routines and Rituals

Every strong culture has routines and rituals that contribute in some way to the cohesion of the social system. Teams also need these to ensure support identity and make concrete contributions  to competitive success. Practice routines are thus part of the team infrastructure. It may be that you want for part of the team culture to be a strong commitment to practice. Some coaches measure player commitment by how much time players spend practicing outside the formal sessions that are limited by Association rules. In some teams a certain amount of "voluntary" practice is expected and failure to meet the expectation is viewed as an indication of poor attitude or lack of support for the team. The design of practice routines varies with the type of sport. For some sports I think it is important for the coach to be the designer and for the players to comply. This is probably most true for sports such as football and basketball where active constant teamwork is integral to the game itself. Sports like tennis, baseball and golf may have more players that have private outside coaches, and this fact can play a role in determining practice routines. In any case it is your job to determine if a player is getting the amount and kinds of practice that is necessary for performance.

A word about outside private coaches may be necessary here. Like your own assistants, volunteers and captains these coaches can be either a great help or a great burden to you. It is crucial to reach out to them and clarify your roles with regard to the player and the team. You are the ultimate voice of the team. The private coach will be primarily interested in the individual player. Your interests are best served by open discussion of how this distribution of responsibilities can work to your mutual advantage. Ultimately, the answer lies in frequent "checking in" with each other. The private coach may have limited opportunity to see the player in competition. You can be his or her eyes on how the player performs under those conditions. The private coach has (we hope) a development plan for the player. He or she can help you to understand that plan and the two of you can agree on how it can be supported by your program. The key is that you both must agree that performance is the final arbiter of what is working and/or needs to be done. If the player is not improving or playing up to potential, something probably has to change in the practice routine.

Rituals during competition can also be helpful. On one championship golf team with which we have worked each player completing the last hole of a round returns to the green to carry the bag of the next player finishing so that player can pay attention to completing the scorecard. This ritual contributes to perceptions of mutual support and demonstrates team cohesion. Rituals also have a potential downside as we have seen with certain rites of passage in some military units and fraternal organizations that become abusive and dangerous. Yes, it is your job to draw the line at this sort of thing. Cheer loudly for routines and rituals that are positive and help build a cohesive team culture, but be cautious about anything that smacks of hazing or is about power for specific team members.

I know of one senior management team of an airline that had a ritual of awarding a fancy toilet seat to the member of the team that had made the biggest blunder during the past quarter. I don't necessarily recommend this sort of thing for a new or frequently changing team but it worked quite well for this team that had spent a number of years working together. Reward rituals that recognize extraordinary contributions to the team are probably a better idea, but remember to only award them if they are deserved. It is better to skip making the award than to cheapen it by giving it for less than extra effort. Healthy kids know the difference between an award that means something and a token without real meaning.

CHAPTER 4   POWER AND OWNERSHIP

Control and Effectiveness

They say that psychology is a science. My professors told me that and I believe it in the same way that people believe their prophets and religious teachings. The trouble even for we who believe is that psychology is a social science. Everything that the social sciences claim to prove is suspect for lots of reasons the researchers among you know very well. In the end the results of all scientific endeavors are suspect when it comes to defining absolute truth. Anyway my studies of psychology and my experience in applying what I have learned have convinced me that there are two psychological factors from which all human behavior derives. Yes, there are effects from physical trauma and growth anomalies but we are working in the realm of "normal" psychology here. The two factors are control and effectiveness (we call it efficacy). Perceptions about these things are what it is all about and most of the work of a good coach is about managing relationships with this in mind.

Many people used to think that things like self esteem were important. I did too at one time but I have never seen a focus on self esteem make a difference where results mattered or really influence the bottom line in any way. The great state of California even created a special social engineering initiative back in the 70's (wasn't the 70's a wonderfully magical time? Okay maybe not) to improve the self esteem of the entire state. At the time I thought that it was not fair to improve the self esteem of people who already had plenty. I even had visions of self esteem fraud perpetrated by those with enough self esteem that might get more of the state's dole and sell it on the black market to states like Mississippi that had to have a real shortage. In the end California had no more idea about how to improve statewide self-esteem than I had so no vast criminal conspiracies were generated and no fairness issues emerged.

My real education about this came a number of years ago when I spent four years consulting with the federal prison system. I found that there was no lack of self esteem among the convicts with whom we worked in our attempts to prevent their return to jail. It turned out that the real problems were bad thinking, lack of character and laziness - not a shortfall of self esteem. The success that we had was in "habilitation" not rehabilitation. With the exception of the true sociopaths the people we were working with had never learned to function in mature, accountable, adult ways. They always felt out of control and incompetent in mainstream living and settled on being victims as the general strategy for dealing with life. I think that coaches deal with the same essential issues. Many crimes against teamwork look a lot like crimes against society and the causes are much the same. The real issue revolves around "Do I have appropriate control and do I think I can do this, not, Am I worthy?"

Strategies for gaining a sense of appropriate control and effectiveness are widely variable. One of my clients had a person, a first-level supervisor, reporting to her who could not seem to get the idea that violations of attendance policies and poor performance by his subordinates should have negative consequences. He consistently failed to discuss expectations with employees and when transgressions occurred his responses were to do nothing or to listen sympathetically to excuses. And he certainly never documented anything. The outcome was predictable and sad.

The subordinate who after a year of employment had never been helped to know what the job was how she was doing and who cared eventually failed in the job. Her failure was not all her fault. The supervisor's failure resulted in the loss of a year of production by a basically capable person. More importantly, it robbed the subordinate of a year of her life that could have been spent building a record of performance. Instead she had a year of poor performance from which she had to recover. We have seen this happen in sports teams as well.

The supervisor's failures to act according to his accountabilities as a supervisor may have roots in his attempts to control others' perceptions of him. He wanted to be liked by people and he reported that being liked was inconsistent with enforcing rules. His being "nice" may have been a successful strategy for gaining a sense of control over people's perceptions of him, but it was clearly inconsistent with his role as a supervisor even though he may have believed that being liked was a measure of effectiveness as a supervisor. Go figure.

Another client had a player with whom she had some history of conflict. Despite the coach's commitment and sincere efforts to learn skills that would prevent such conflict, the player was absolutely unwilling to accept the possibility that a new relationship could be forged. It appears that to take the risk to reach out or accept the overtures of the coach would represent a destruction of her defenses against further hurt, a loss of control. Furthermore, her perceived effectiveness as a person would be at risk if she were to admit to having a role in creating the conflict. The player ended up leaving the team under uncomfortable circumstances. Both the coach and the player lost something in that one.

In another case a player approached us asking if we could help with gaining release from the team. The reasons given reflected more mature thinking in that there was no criticism of the coach only the assertion that what was expected did not happen. Probing revealed some coach behaviors that fell short of expectations, but that was not given as the reason. The message was. "I made a mistake in choosing this program and think that I can perform better in a different one." There is no victim here, only a person who admits to an error in judgment and wants to correct it.

There may have been more going on there but this example illustrates the difference between running away from something with no sense of accountability and running toward something with a commitment to improvement.

So how can a coach or manager influence these critical factors? The key is in answering three questions for every member of the team on a very frequent basis. Each of us brings these questions to the job every day and in some ways many times a day. They are, **"What's my job?" "How am I doing?"** and **"Who cares?"**

The answer to the first is critical because knowledge about goals, expectations and standards is a source of power to achieve. Goals imply authority. Goals without authority are empty wishes. Goals without both authority and measurement are a joke. I have seen many an employee chuckle at the exhortations of management to get things done when the rank and file knew clearly that they had no authority or had no idea what getting things done meant. You can rest assured that the signs around the workplace that say, "Make It Happen!" generate more sarcastic questions about what "It" is and how we will know when it has happened than they do energetic performance.

Feedback, which answers the second question, may be the single most important tool that any person has in building a trusting and honest relationship with another. Its absence certainly amounts to deception at worse and lack of concern for the relationship at best. There is specific direction on how to give feedback in the section on "I Messages." In general, feedback, if it is to be useful and supportive, has to inform and not punish. When done properly it even contributes to answering the third question. Only people who care will give useful, informative feedback.

Caring is absolutely necessary. It is a source of "power with" rather than "power over." You have to like them to lead them is a fair thing to say. If you don't like them the answer to the third question (Who cares?) will be, "I don't know but it surely isn't me." The good news is that you are more able to like people whom you manage and lead well.

I hope it goes without saying that you should avoid recruiting people that you really don't like. You do have to trust your gut about some things and this may be one of the most important. Eddie Haskell was a polite and well-behaved young man but your gut would tell you something was not quite right about that fellow. Even if you had no idea how he acted when with Wally and the Beaver, you would know that you should not trust him. Mrs. Cleaver knew it, too.

Anyway, caring is crucial and there are many ways in which it shows. I must digress here to give you a short list of ways that people show how they care. It may not be an obvious list so I will have to explain it a bit. Bear with me. This is important.

There are several things that you can do to provide the answer to the "Who cares?" question. Each is important in its own right but they also form a kind of hierarchical system of behavior that has some synergy.

1. Show Up. Woody Allen was right. It is 80% of everything. It means things as simple as being on time and honoring appointments to things more difficult like being there when a player is suffering the slings and arrows of outrageous fortune and, for a while, needs someone who will not judge. It means being there when they practice and when they play. It 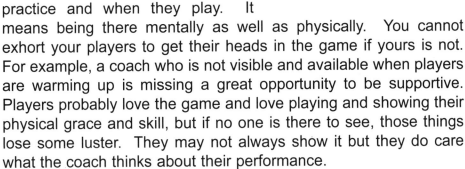 means being there mentally as well as physically. You cannot exhort your players to get their heads in the game if yours is not. For example, a coach who is not visible and available when players are warming up is missing a great opportunity to be supportive. Players probably love the game and love playing and showing their physical grace and skill, but if no one is there to see, those things lose some luster. They may not always show it but they do care what the coach thinks about their performance.

Coaches can often do a lot to cement relationships and show caring by doing some non-sport activities with players during free time on the road.   One coach I know goes shopping with players. Apparently women think that shopping for something other than tools is a recreational activity. Beats me where that comes from.

Anyway the players think that it is "cool" that the coach goes with them. This sort of shared experience can go a long way toward strengthening relationships within the team, but you have to be there to share it.

2. Pay Attention.   Keep your eyes and ears and whatever sixth sense you have open and receptive   at   all   times. Furthermore practice some active listening so that players know that you are paying attention.   Paying attention is one of the most fundamental ways in which humans of every ilk show that they care about another person.   There may be nothing more important to showing that you care. The withdrawal of attention is, in fact, used as punishment in a number of ways.   In English public school (private school to Americans) a common form of severe punishment was called "being sent to Coventry" which equated with being ignored completely. For us humans being ignored can be worse than being cursed. At least a curse recognizes that we exist.

Paying attention is an active process. I cannot imagine that you have not had some exposure to active listening skills in your own education. It is so very commonly understood as a basic skill for effective communication that every school teaches it at some point. Some of its power derives from the fact that it serves both the listener and the speaker. While the speaker gets verification that he or she has been heard, the listener gets a better understanding of what is going on and has time to formulate an effective response. Many people, like me for example, are simply too quick to respond. We finish the other person's thoughts or provide an answer before there is a question. It is disrespectful and builds barriers to communication rather than bridges.

Active listening also gets you information about the emotional subtext of what is being said. The word content will sometimes be at odds with the feelings going on in the person. Emotions are communicated through multiple channels. If you pay attention to what the person is doing and saying you can get information from body language, facial expressions and voice tones as well as from verbal contents.

Perhaps the most important thing about active listening is that it requires patience. Let people finish and then let them know that you have heard and want to be sure that you have heard what is truly being said. Summarize content, reflect emotions and ask for clarification if you need it. If you are not going to do these things, for heaven's sake don't pretend to be listening. Set another time when you can fully pay attention and show up at that time.

3. Add Value. Work to ensure that everything you do as Coach helps players to grow and enables them to perform up to their potential. You show by the quality of your behavior that you care about the team and about individual players. I   have seen coaches and managers that want all of the responsibility for performance to be on the heads of the players and employees. In the sense that only the player plays the game that is true, but that does not get you off the hook.

Your actual and symbolic role as parent figure makes you responsible for the environment in which players execute their responsibilities for performance on the field, court, course, etc. While you may not have the power to make talent come alive during competition you can certainly crush talent by your lack of caring about the player and his or her performance. Adding value has aspects from both axes of the 9, 9 Grid.

Forge a climate in which there is clear understanding of goals and expectations. Let there be no doubt that you and the team have standards that will be met and make sure that those standards contribute to excellence in performance and are not just a way for you to impose a personal value system on the players. One of the things that have a chilling effect on individual and team performance is a standard that is outdated or serves no function in a current situation. There is a great story that made the rounds during the heyday of the Total Quality Management movement about cutting the pot roast. It is told that a woman was in the habit of cutting the ends from a pot roast whenever she prepared one. When asked by her daughter why she did that, the woman replied that it was a practice handed down from her mother. To make what can be a long story short it turned out that the originator of the practice performed the cuts because her roasting pan was too small to accommodate the entire roast. The practice of cutting had survived even though there was no longer any need since later generations had larger pans.

Adding value means doing what is helpful, supportive and enables players to get the job done. It is about the job getting done in the best way possible. No standard or practice is of much value if it must be overcome in order to get optimal performance. I have seen coaches and managers deliberately create obstacles so that their people could learn from the process of overcoming them. What's up with that? Isn't the game demanding enough in itself? Are not the barriers to winning sufficiently formidable to be worth your focus? Get over yourself. Adding value may mean designing training work that accurately simulates game conditions but the work must be an accurate simulation of the game, not some artificial problem intended to teach some obscure lesson. Life and the game itself will provide enough opportunities and requirements for building skill and character.

Adding value can also be in terms of compensation and incentives.

We know that compensation is necessary in order to maintain minimal levels of performance and we know that incentives can support extra effort. Provide as much of both as you can without going overboard. One of the things that I have learned in the capital workplace is that there is a critical relationship between price and perceived value. If I am overpaid I am just as likely to under-perform as if I were underpaid. Sufficient compensation (scholarships and legal perks) that meets reasonable expectations is necessary. Work on this during recruiting and don't overpay just because you get seduced by player potential or personality.

Meaningful incentives tied to real performance improvements and/or personal and team achievements will support motivation. Don't overdo them. Save incentives for the things that require the most support. If you provide incentives for everything they will lose their power and you will find yourself in an upward value spiral such that you have to continually sweeten the pot in order for the incentives to have the desired effect.

Adding value means working to ensure that the players on your payroll have the best student-athlete experience possible. Ask yourself every time you are about to do or say something, "How will this contribute to that great experience?" If it doesn't help them to play better or to grow emotionally and thus feel better about themselves and their performance then don't do it or do it differently.

REMEMBER THAT IT IS NOT ABOUT YOU. IT IS ABOUT THEM. YOU DON'T COACH A SPORT, YOU COACH PEOPLE .

Being clear about what the job is, giving good feedback so that people know how they are doing and showing that you care creates the ideal climate for performance. In an appropriate climate, people take responsibility for their own actions, opinions, feelings and attitudes. The resulting freedom and energy empower them. People learn to convert blame to problem analysis and renewed goal commitment. Conflicts are more easily resolved; decisions and actions become are seldom surprising in negative ways. People recognize that cooperation and collaboration reap great individual and organizational rewards even thought the payoffs may come more slowly.

There are a number of useful ways to view and understand the dynamics of human relationships. I choose to see them in terms of the deals we make - the contracts with others that we make in order to maintain a sense of personal control and effectiveness. I have not seen a situation that could not be understood from this perspective, so I think of the relationships in and around your team in that way as well. You might immediately recognize that if this "contract" perspective is valid then healthy relationships must involve the perception of a fair exchange of value. I'll grant you that some of these perceptions can seem strange. The contract to which an abused spouse appears to agree is not my cup of tea, but it seems to serve some. The deal that some employees sign up for that gets them long hours, verbal abuse and minimal pay is not attractive to me, but I have found that humans are able to perceive value in a wide variety of situations where I would not.

Athletes too will accept apparently uncomfortable situations for the opportunity to play for a certain school or coach or in order to stay close to mom, the significant other or whatever. I am not suggesting that the contract has to have anything specific in it. It just needs to be clearly understood and maintained. Change in the provisions of the deal is up to the parties. From the coach's perspective it would be good to negotiate deals for top talent at the least cost possible to the school and the coach. From the player perspective it is reasonable to look for as much money and legal perks as can be had for the promise and delivery of excellent performance.

There is a wealth of formal literature about these sorts of relationship contracts. I have read most of it so that I could reinforce my beliefs about how things work among humans. If you want to understand the nuts and bolts of psychological contracts in organizations you can get the book by Dr. Denise Rousseau of Carnegie Mellon University from any academic bookstore or online outlet.

Anyway, no matter what the deal is it has to be perceived as fair by both sides and it must be actively maintained because it will change over time as experience is gained and expectations change. Hence the importance of communication and why verbal interaction plays such an important role in coaching. Communication is a coach's primary tool. There are a few absolute do's and don'ts that you can follow that will help.

An Appropriate Balance of Power

This is crucial if you are going to be an effective coach/parent. That essentially means that you keep most of the power in your hands. I have seen coaches that want to be liked or respected so much that they give players way too much power. There are several ways in which they do this. The first is in terms of attitude and personal needs.

It is common for us as humans to make concessions of power in order to relate with another person in the way that we want to. We do it on the job where we soften bad news so that we don't anger the boss. We do in during dating rituals so that we can move around the "bases" (Do people still talk that way?) or get over. We do it in the context of family as spouses and as children as we learn what pushes the buttons of partners and parents. In all of these cases we are allowing another person to have some kind of power in order to meet a need of ours.

We don't care at the time that we are planting land mines in the landscape of our relationship when we do this. What is important is that we get to feel the way we want to at the moment and not make the other person angry. Please get this. You have never "made" someone else feel anything unless you have touched the person physically. Anger does tend to follow pain so if you smack someone upside the head you can generally expect anger if they survive. But, you can no more make someone be angry than you can make someone love you. You can do many things that can have an impact on emotions but there is never a reliable cause and effect between what you do and the actual emotions the other person experiences.

Yes, you can provoke somewhat predictable responses if you have a history with a person that taught you how they are likely to react but that is manipulation or button pushing. The outcomes of attempts at manipulation are not absolutely predictable because the other party may choose to be mature enough to escape being manipulated at any time.

You stay "clean" in relationships by maintaining and meeting moral and ethical standards that are aimed at supporting and helping others in the most grown up ways possible. More importantly, you avoid problems by open discussion of these standards from the beginning of your association with the person/player or fellow coach.

An issue that comes up quite a bit is how decisions should be made. There are those that suggest you should make all of the decisions affecting the team and there are those that suggest you should involve players. They are both right. This is really question of the right distribution of power.

Most decisions about the team should be in your hands because you have most of the accountability but there are different ways to go about making decisions. Your job is to choose the process well. You can make the decision and announce it to the team. You can ask for input from the team and then make the decision or you can turn the decision over to the team to make. And there are options within this range for how you handle the process.

For example, you can present the problem or question to the team and ask for ideas. You can present the problem along with a list of options that may or may not be expanded by the team. You can even present a set of circumstances to the team and ask them to define the problem, develop solutions and choose a course of action. The amount of authority you give to the team is what varies in these options.

For me the important thing to consider when thinking about distributing authority is whether or not the integrity and cohesion of the team is at stake. If there is any chance that the team image or ability to perform can be affected negatively then you probably want to keep the final authority in your own hands. For anything else turn it over. It will help players to grow and keep you out of unnecessary detail. I think that you will want to err on the side of distributing accountability. It may bite you on the posterior but may also turn out to help a player grow in ways that are truly important.

One coach I know struggled with deciding how players should dress for a team photo that would be used for the media guide. She had received input from an advisor that the players should be involved in the decision but was still concerned about what the players might choose. Was the integrity of the team at stake in this one? The answer is yes. The very public image that the team presents reflects not only on the team but on the institution as well and certainly on the coach. This is decision that is made easier by having a standard in place with regard to image. Here the coach had to keep and exercise her veto power if necessary after getting input from players. It might have been okay for the coach to get input, choose some options, present the options to the team as the only choices available and let them choose. That could get you the best of both worlds but it will probably be seen by some as the coach making the decision. Too bad, there is too much at stake to turn this one completely over.

I have actually seen a media guide that presented an awful picture of a team. The dress was much too casual and did not show the degree of class that the reputation of the school called for. It did not serve the team or the school well and I trace that to the fact that the decision was made by the players and not the coach.

The secret to using the power of your position well is that you are never seen using it solely for your own convenience or personal agenda. Your personal likes and dislikes are not a sufficient basis for decisions except when they are backed up by something greater. You are an agent of the organization whose job it is to meet organization goals. Those goals are what provide the basis for your authority to choose. Those goals also include things that the players and you want as well so there should not be a lot of problem with that.

Be the One with the Questions

You have power as a result of your position and the contracts that you have made. Your power is under constant assault. It's not that players set out to undermine your authority or rob you of your role. They will unconsciously try to steal power in order to meet their own needs for control and a sense of effectiveness. Your mission, Mr. Phelps, is to help them to meet their needs without giving up your legitimate role and the power required to fulfill it. Your primary weapon in this battle is the art of inquiry.

It is a given that the person with the questions is the one with the greater power in any verbal exchange. You have all seen many scenes in police dramas on television where the police affirm that they are the ones who will be asking the questions. Even when they do not assert themselves as the questioners they will ignore questions from witnesses and suspects unless the answer serves their investigation in some way. I am not suggesting that you behave in that way, only that you get the point that the one with the questions is the more powerful in the exchange. Power, of course, must be used judiciously in order to be maintained.

While the police may be trying to uncover facts and perceptions that may be hidden from them you are not. Your questions will have to do with your genuine curiosity about what is going on with the other person. You are always asking because you want to help in the best way possible and the information you seek will enable you to be supportive. As it turns out you also get the added benefits of maintaining your appropriate power and getting time to sort out how to interact in a way that truly is helpful and supportive.

Another example is the psychotherapist's practice of answering questions with questions. We often make fun of this behavior and characters in film often model it when they are protecting deep dark secrets. The fact is that the therapist is making sure that the focus of the discussion stays on the client. There is no value in shifting it to the therapist or to the coach for that matter. Remember, it is about them not about you so you must, like the therapist, keep the focus where it will do the most good.

Another important and valuable thing that you can generate with questions is the "teachable moment." If you can stumble upon an actual desire to learn something, you can leap to the occasion and become the teacher that you have longed to be. Teachable moments are very hard to force into being so you have to catch them when they pop up and they pop up way less than you will want them to. They are like the marble-sized nuggets of gold that early prospectors found that led to indulgence in the famous wine, women and song of legend and police blotter fame. Rejoice in them and treat them with the reverence that they deserve.

Lots of bang for the buck in these questions but remember that any other agenda that you may have besides help and support will be visible and also cost you in terms of lost power and influence. Right now you may be feeling some of the tremendous weight of responsibility of which I spoke earlier, but fear not. I make much of what is important because I feel that strongly about it. I am also guilty of expecting a great deal from you because I believe that you are up to the challenge.

There are obvious types of questions that players will ask to which you must respond with a question in order to maintain appropriate power and to actually help the situation. Be aware of these and be prepared to respond to them with a question of your own.

The "whyne"

This is normally a question that begins with the word "why" and is designed as a challenge to some decision or policy or aspect of reality with which the player is not

happy. It is often delivered with the familiar whine of the preadolescent child. Examples are the "Why do we, Why don't they, Why must I, and Why can't we questions that have the effect of challenge. A response that will turn aside the challenge and maintain the balance of power is wanted here. For example, "How will it help if we didn't (or they didn't, or you mustn't or you could)? If you can find out what is behind the question you may actually be able to help the player solve the problem without changing a policy or decision.

The "When" and "Where" Setup

Very close to the whyne but with the elements of time and location included. "When/Where will we, When/Where can I, When/Where will they" and others are all openings that should trigger your warning lights. Even if the question is a sincere request for information about a schedule, for example, you must inquire to find out more. The player may be trying to figure a way to avoid a scheduled workout, practice or meeting and is working on getting you to support their absence. The player may also have a good idea about an improvement to a schedule and wants an opportunity to offer it without fear of ridicule or retribution. Regardless of the specific reason the question is probably a setup to enable a statement to be made or a follow-up rhetorical question that will leave you inescapably trapped by your own words.

Beyond the obvious warning signs above you must view every conversation opener from a player as both a threat to the balance of power and an opportunity to create a teachable moment. Hence, a question must be your first response to almost anything that a player says to you.

It cannot be a sarcastic question and should never be a "why" question. It is a question to gain clear or sufficient information so that you can be helpful and supportive. Your question must be aimed at getting you the information that you need to provide the right information in the right amounts to which the player has a right. Avoid rhetorical questions that are actually statements or evaluations. For example, "What made you choose such an impossible shot?" is an evaluative statement despite the question mark at the end. Don't do this sort of questioning. It will work better to say something like, "What made you choose that shot?"

Even that question may produce a defense since it questions motive but if you manage your tone well, you can get to the bottom of the thought process that produced the (absolutely unbelievably stupid) behavior you witnessed. It is all about purity in your motives and discipline. You cannot want to hurt. If you do you will. It is as simple as that. You can maintain a balance of power by assuming that there is more that you can know and you have a right to know it or you can upset the balance by putting a player down, starting with an evaluation or ignoring her or him.

Notice that I said it is harmful to start with an evaluation not that you must avoid evaluation altogether. Evaluation is an integral part of your job. As parent you must sometimes judge. I only ask that you do it well. Evaluation requires framing. Framing means that you have a legitimate reason for a given type of evaluation.   For example, evaluation can be framed by an explicit clause in your contract with players or as part of well-designed feedback.

Your demand for the right to offer evaluation of player performance will probably have to be negotiated in some situations and not in others.   Athletes in sports where the emphasis is greater on individual performance such as tennis, golf and track and field are, in my experience, less likely to want or accept unsolicited evaluation. Work this out with them during the recruiting and orientation period or you will be sorry that you did not.

Never Argue

I can think of no situation in which it serves anyone for you to engage in an argument with a player. Your job is to get the facts, clarify the perceptions,
communicate expectations and feedback, render judgments and

make decisions. None of these require you to argue with players. Even if you were to win all of your arguments you would do so at the cost of your respectability. "Reasoning" with a player must mean helping her or him to be clear about what they think, feel and want and then supporting their good decisions while discouraging their poor ones. To do anything else will earn you more ownership of the player's life than you ever want.

Argument is a contest. You have no need to contest with your players. Your word is final and you earn the right to invoke your absolute right to the final word by being trusted as a person, respected as a reliable authority and as a model for moral and ethical behavior. If you find yourself arguing recognize this as a symptom of a trust or respect problem. Of course it may also be that you have an immature jerk on your team that can't seem to get it through that thick adolescent skull that you are the boss -- just kidding - a little. I was getting a bit evangelical there and thought some levity might help.

Anyway, your legitimate status gives you the essential authority and accountability you <u>earn</u> the rest of the stuff you need to be a leader and effective manager.

Problem Ownership

There is another very important reason that questions are your friend. They help you to ensure that there is no confusion about problem ownership. Many people who have learned the wily ways of victimhood (I made up that word) are really good at handing off responsibility to others. We have all done it at various times in our lives. It is a common childhood behavior that we grow out of as we mature. Some do not mature as rapidly as others. The player was not late for practice because you didn't arrange transportation. The player was late for practice because the player did not take care of his or her need to get there.

Sometimes they even try to transfer responsibility to inanimate objects. "My alarm did not go off this morning." The fact that the alarm was not set might have had something to do with that so you might want to inquire into how the player normally ensures that the alarm is properly set and working. The question helps to make it clear that the player, not the alarm clock, owns the problem.

You can rest assured that no one works on problems that they do not own in some way. Failure to meet standards or follow rules is a problem and the owner is the one who failed. If the standards and/or rules have not been communicated or are unreasonable, then management (that's you) owns the problem. If you have done your job in communicating and reinforcing the importance of standards the player owns the problem. Questioning will help you to ensure that everyone is clear from whom the solution must come.

I would like to be more specific about the kind of questioning that is helpful here but I cannot. Each situation will call for a different focus.

Questions may begin in a variety of ways.

> "Are you suggesting…"
> "Do you mean…"
> "What is it that you expect?"
> "How do you want this to come out?"
> "Will you please help me to understand…"
> "In what way can I help you to..."
> "Will you share with me…"
> "What would you like me to do
>   with/about that?"

It all depends upon what will serve best to reveal the real agenda of the player so you can help him or her solve the problem.

Use "I" Messages

The flip side of questions is opening statements. You will often be the one that is initiating communication. In addition, it may not be appropriate for you to start out with a question. You may want to just get to the point by starting a dialogue with your thoughts and feelings about something.

Even if you have an agreement that permits you to offer evaluation you will be smart to frame it as part of useful feedback. Unvarnished evaluations of people in any situation are seldom accepted and can produce nasty responses. Good coaches are good models and one of the things that you must model is effective communication. There are two reasons for learning just a few very important things. The first is that you must be a model of good stuff or you will either have no credibility or end up modeling something less desirable. The second is that you cannot maintain appropriate power in your relationships without the right behavior.

"I" messages have been taught as a tool for effective communication for many years. They are essentially a method for avoiding direct confrontation or subsequent escalation of conflict. "I" messages have their greatest impact when used to deliver positive feedback. Few of the problems associated with their misuse will accrue from using them to say how what another person did was good or helpful and you feel good about it. They are good as a framing mechanism for feedback that could be confrontational as well. . Of course, like all tools they can be used badly. Don't you hate that? I know that I do. I want things that are perfect and work all the time and require virtually no effort on my part and produce even better outcomes than I had imagined. Yeah, right. That's going to happen.

More realistically we grown up folks realize that a potentially powerful tool will have potential power for good and for ill. Sorry, that's the way it is so pay attention to how to make sure you don't misuse this tool. There are several things to watch for. First I will describe the type of "I" message I am suggesting that you use and then discuss the caveats.

The basic key to an "I" message is that it uses the pronoun I more than the pronoun you. This is intended to ensure clear ownership of what is being said and avoid sounding like an accusation. There are normally three parts to the message and I add a fourth that I think helps to avoid misuse. "I" messages are usually structured in the following manner: "When you (exhibit or neglect to exhibit a certain behavior), I feel (a certain feeling) because (describe actual impact on performance, rule that has been broken, agreement violated or standard not met) and I want (say what you want)." The order of the elements can be different so long as it makes sense. Let's look at each part to see how it can be helpful (or not) to our purpose of good communication.

"When you..." The key here is to be very specific about observable behavior. It must be something that was actually done or said. Speculation or guesswork is of no use here. Some critics of the use of I messages will point out that we are beginning with the pronoun "you." We are. The fact is that the message is about the other person's behavior or lack of it so this is unavoidable. The "I" part comes in the next segment of the message. Since we are so close to accusation when we use "you" in the message, you must be really accurate about the behavior (or lack) or you will turn this valuable tool into a boomerang in a New York minute.

"I feel..." This is an important part for you. It ensures that you express ownership of your state of mind by acknowledging your emotions. And it can be misused in two ways. First just because you couple the feelings you are having with the behavior you have described does not mean that the other person is accountable for your feelings. He or she is in no way responsible for taking care of your feelings for you. This acknowledgement is for you. It makes you honest with yourself about what you are feeling if you get in the habit of saying how you feel. It can be helpful information for the other person as a clarification of your reaction to their behavior. When he or she fails to show up for practice and does not call, it irritates you and makes you more likely to include the fact in your evaluations of his or her performance and you will be evaluating performance.

"Because..." Here we get the reason for your emotion. It is not just the behavior. Behavior in itself is neutral. It is the effects of the behavior that matter and here you have to be really honest and factual about the effects. If you manufacture impact you will be discovered and it will destroy your credibility as a source of feedback. So, if absence from practice irritates you it should be for a reason such as the fact that such absences are a waste of talent that will not develop without practice. It is disrespectful to oneself to let talent go to waste and that can irritate any coach. The impact could also be that it causes other players to lodge complaints of favoritism with you or to harbor resentments toward you for perceived favoritism.

"I want..." This is the part that I add to ensure that you don't imply that the other person must find some magical way to alleviate your feelings. It has to be about something of importance to the team. In this world you have to ask for what you want. You may get some things purely by accident but if you expect them and do nothing to get them you will be nearly always disappointed. What you want from other people is usually a change in behavior or the delivery on a promise made or something like that. It will always involve some behavior on the part of the other person so be very careful what you ask for - you might get it.

In our example of the coach who is irritated when the player misses practice because it is a waste of talent and disrespectful of self, what may be wanted is for the player to renew his or her commitment to practice and actually show up without fail for the remainder of his or her life. Well, maybe not that long, but certainly long enough to demonstrate that the commitment is real and comes from a mature person. The payoff in compliance with the coach's authoritative request comes in several forms. It can mitigate negative evaluation of the player's performance. It can also eliminate complaints from other players. Only players with really exceptional records of achievement and performance whose work ethic ensures that they will make up any lost practice time can blow off scheduled team practice. No player can do it in a sport where teamwork during competition is crucial (football, basketball, soccer, water polo, lacrosse, etc.).

There is another type of message that does not call for the use of any pronouns at all. The argument for using this message type is that there are situations where your feelings are not likely to be a problem for you so you don't have to work at your own awareness of them. Furthermore there are some messages that can only come from you since you hold the authority to enforce rules.

These situations are about clear and simple violations of previously established agreements, standards, and rules or understood boundaries. Conscious, unexcused failure to honor any of these is unacceptable and the player needs to get that message if he or she is going to be an effective member of the team. An example may be something like, "Unexcused absence from practice is unacceptable. Don't let it happen again if you want to remain on the team." Whereas the former type of message made ownership and state of mind clear this one only states the crime and the punishment. This can be a very useful corrective message for any of your brighter players who have a tendency to want to negotiate everything. Sometimes they need to get the message that there will be no discussion and there will be consequences for failure to meet expectations.

There is another type of feedback that is less personal and has power in its own right. There is feedback that is purely informative. The sales figures for the week or performance statistics from a tournament provide information about performance. It is feedback that comes directly from performance. It may be the most useful performance-related information that a player can get because it has tremendous value for defining good performance goals. Realistic targets for improvement can come only from factual information about current levels of performance.

Something to remember about informative feedback is that timing is crucial. Whereas "I" messages and corrective feedback are best delivered as immediately after the infraction as possible informative feedback is best used when planning performance. There are several reasons for this. Perhaps the most important is that feedback from performance will provoke a committed person to act, to improve, to change something. How to act and what to change is better discussed in closer proximity to the next performance event. Talking about it immediately after the last performance event can lead to nothing more than frustration growing out of not being able to do anything about getting better.

Turn "Problem Talk" into "Possibility Talk"

At the risk of sounding a bit cliché you really must help kids to treat obstacles and problems in ways that are useful and effective. Dwelling on difficulties has never helped anyone to achieve anything. It is the possibilities that define our goals and help to energize us to act in positive self-affirming ways.

Kids often love drama. Very few people in the world have children like those on 7th Heaven. Who are those kids anyway? They are certainly not human. I think that show probably started out as a science fiction piece that got altered at the last minute. Anyway, normal kids will often tend to get caught up in the seriousness of their difficulties that they fail to see the opportunities before them. Help them to see.

Try this simple model for personal problem solving. When a player comes to you with a problem, ask questions to determine what **goal** the player has related to the situation or problem. Next explore the **reality** surrounding the situation including the barriers to achieving the goal and the enabling circumstances that exist. Then help him or her to brainstorm a list of **options** that will result in meeting the goal. Last urge the player to **choose** an option and identify the first action steps necessary to get moving in the right direction.

I know that you will be tempted to suggest solutions to their problems but don't do it unless specifically asked. As soon as you devise the solution you own the problem and you certainly don't want to go there. Your "wise counsel" will be deeply appreciated if you stay out of the problem and stay engaged as a guide through the problem-solving process.

CHAPTER 5   FAIR DOESN'T MEAN EQUAL

So, What is Fair Anyway?

A close look at nature, history and
any group of people tells us that equality is not part of the design of
our universe. That doesn't keep us from thinking that equality and
fairness are the same thing.   The problem is that equal is a
measurement and the outcomes of measurement are always
dependent upon the standards, tools and methods used to
measure. When we complain about things not being equal, and we
all do at some time, we are applying a standard, tool and method we
have chosen for the particular situation. We only make fair and
equal the same by constructing standards and methods that define
them that way. While it is arguable that equality can be a scientific
measure - four quarts is always equal to one gallon - fairness is
never so easily determined. It is a subjective measure.

As coaches, you will certainly be tested from time to time by your
players who resent your decisions as being "unfair". The most
strident advocates for fairness are seldom the best or star players.
Am I right? Of course I am. The best players are not equal with the
others in terms of any number of factors that make their performance
measurably better. They have more talent or they put more effort into
practice or they are more mature and they resent any attempt to say
that their scholarship size or the attention they get from boosters or
the media or the coach is not fair. They earned it.

Well folks, if you haven't figured it out already, fair does not mean equal unless you're a socialist or my mother dividing up cookies between me and my brother when I was growing up in Southern Illinois. In fact, quite the opposite is true. I am an "older" man with a bad ticker, a cholesterol problem, and thirty pounds of baggage that no matter how many times I try to lose it, keeps on finding me like the IRS. I will never be a multi-millionaire professional athlete. Is this "fair?" Not in my mind. I want to be equal with slender wealthy people who have no health problems and play "A" level tennis at the local club. This is not, however, a fairness problem. It is a get over yourself problem.

If you make decisions based on everyone being equal, it would be inherently unfair. For example, if you have a team member who consistently outperforms everyone else on the team he or she also has the most to gain or lose if the team succeeds or fails. Conversely, a team member who underperforms or shows no effort has nothing to lose if the team fails - to this type of person; there may be very little sense of perceived "gain" except perhaps by bringing everyone else down to the same low performance level. To provide the same level of scholarship support to both players in the name of being equal would be patently unfair to the first player and to the team.

Humorist Wayne Allred has observed that if life were fair horses would ride half the time. Life is not fair. Fairness, like justice, character and the ability to wear clothes designed for people with eating disorders is something that you have to work at. One of the myths that makes this work especially hard is that fair means equal. Fair and equal are overlapping sets of things. Sometimes fairness demands equality and sometimes it demands difference. If you think for a moment, I am sure that you will be able to come up with some examples. Take the time to write them down. You may need them when a player accuses you of favoritism. Just in case you cannot, here are some to think about.

In any athletic contest, fair does mean equal when you are talking about the common conditions and circumstances under which both teams play. Each team plays on the same field with the same rules and the same weather and the same league administration. The teams do not, however have the same players. If fair were equal the best players and/or the worst players would play for every team. That would make the contest more equal.

If fair and equal were the same, work standards in any situation would be segmented according to a narrowly defined range of abilities. That means that people with say an IQ of 105 to 110 who are right-handed, between 5 feet 8 inches and 5 feet 10 inches tall and weighing between 160 and 170 pounds would have one standard and people with an IQ of 111 to 116 who are left-handed, between 5 feet 11 inches and 6 feet tall weighing between 175 and 185 pounds would have a different standard. The same work standards for all does not fairly reflect the lack of equality among the people. Fat chance that will ever happen.

I am reminded of the made-famous-by-Hollywood story of Rudy, the kid at Notre Dame who was completely unqualified by virtue of size and talent to play varsity football. Despite his not being given the obvious tools of a football player, he gave extraordinary effort toward his dream of playing for Notre Dame and eventually was able to play in a game and contribute to a victory - or so the story goes. Rudy did not become famous because the system was managed to ensure that he had an equal chance to play. Notre Dame ain't Little League. Rudy made the movies because he worked so incredibly hard as a person to find ways to contribute to the team's success. He never had an equal chance to play; he created the chance to play. Was that fair? You bet it was. It was fair because the opportunity existed for a person to expend extraordinary effort and personal sacrifice such that he overcame not being equal. The existence of opportunity is what makes things fair, not the guarantee of success.

Here is another one. There is a ton of research that shows that attractive people have a distinct advantage in the world. They are rated better in job interviews and more likely to get offered the job than an equally qualified unattractive person. They get more dates or at least get more offers. They tend to earn more money. They get better performance evaluations. They have a better chance at a career in sports broadcasting after they retire from competition. That may not seem fair and heaven knows that we do all sorts of things to create the impression that attractiveness does not matter, but only a figuratively blind fool would suggest that anything we do can remove this bias from human interactions. We are not equal and there is no way to manipulate or bureaucratize the world to remove the bias associated with this inequity. So, pretty people get more opportunity but in the end they have to be able to put the right number of points on the board. That is when it gets fair. Since there aren't enough pretty people to make teams, some of the rest of us get a chance too and our performance is what gets us into the hall of fame, not our looks.

We are not equally gifted as people and we will not all have the same experiences in our work and play. If fair and equal were the same then all of the students on campus should be given a tryout for the team regardless of past record or experience. Not going to happen. We select and we screen and we exercise bias and that is the way it is and the way it should be in a manageable world.

This doesn't mean that we don't have to work at treating people fairly. We most certainly do. All players who make the team should be given the same standards against which they are measured. Of course those standards should be broad and minimal enough to apply to the realistic range of abilities that comprise a team. There may be higher specific standards (expectations and goals) used to measure performance of your better players, but that is a matter between you and the player. It is a subject of individual goal-setting and evaluation.

All players should have equal access to equipment, coaching and practice. That does not mean that the coach has to manage the system to push these things at people who do nothing to seek them on their own. One of the sad but true things about life is that you get very little of what you do not ask for in some way. Players and coaches must meet in the middle somewhere. Of course the middle of the road is where the heavy traffic is. You are still likely to be accused of favoritism by some. Really good players often enjoy being treated as favorites. Really great players do not. They know what damage is possible from a lack of fairness.

I like asking players who charge a coach with favoritism what they are being deprived of as a result. I have yet to find a player who complains of being deprived in any way at all. What they object to is not what they miss but what another seems to be getting and it is usually the coach's attention in some way. It may also be relief from some responsibility such as workouts or practice. If it is a matter of relief from responsibility then you do have a problem. Showing up or meeting clear responsibilities are standards that you should apply to everyone. At the college level players have to suck it up and play by the rules just as much as everyone else. If there is some extenuating circumstance that applies to one player you will have to either let the rest of the team in on it so that they can agree to an exception or live with the consequences of perceived favoritism.

Coaches are encouraged by an overall system that values winning to give lots of attention to players that can and do contribute to victory. They are also encouraged by their nature as humans to give attention to those who give it to them as well as to those who are just plain more likable. Players who "suck up" also get more of a coach's time even if that time is spent trying to discourage the sucking up. What is never known by the complaining player is exactly how the coach's time is being used by the "privileged" player. If you give attention to every player as an individual in some way you can mitigate the perceptions of favoritism. For large team sports this can be a real challenge and you may have to use assistants and volunteers to help. They can find out the extent to which your personal attention is needed to help an individual player.

Great coaches also make time for other players because it is good coaching to care for all of your players sufficiently. Remember they need to know what the job is, how they are doing and who cares. It is you who must care and you have to show it. You will have a few introverts on the team from time to time that need some initial outreach to establish a good relationship but introverted or not each player is obliged to do some reaching out as well.

Communicate the expectation that players will come to you with any questions or concerns that they may have and the standard that failure to come to you first with any problem about you is a rule violation. If you have any reason to think that players may fear you in any way or fear punishment for questioning you in any way, you can offer to have a "fair witness" present during any meeting. The fair witness should be of the player's choosing and acceptable to you. In truth there may come a time when you will be the one who wants a third party present to prevent any misreporting of what transpired. I hope that it does not come to that, but we live in a harsh world where people sometimes set out to do harm to others.

You will also have the occasional player that you simply do not like as a person. Get over that one. If they play well and contribute to the team and don't do anything to damage morale or cohesiveness, you must find a way to get along. Frankly you probably need to find a way to like the kid. As the more mature adult (we hope) in the relationship it is incumbent on you to take the initiative to improve your perceptions of this person. You must engage, explore, question, disclose feelings and accurately describe expectations. If you have done all that and it still doesn't work out you might have to help the player seek success with another team. Without your support he or she is unlikely to be successful with you. It would be wrong to smother talent in a situation where it won't be brought out because you can't get past personal dislike of a player. The discussion of trust in the next chapter may help you with this.

Coaching/Player Types

Any group larger than one will be made up of different types of people. Your team will be made up of various personalities (including you) that change with time or from moment to moment depending on the situation at hand. I am not much of a fan of putting people in categories or types according to predictable personality traits. The assignment of types encourages me to make predictions about behavior that simply do not come true enough to be helpful in any way. I prefer to think in terms of recognizing that people will do what works to help them to maintain control and feel effective. Helping coaches to put their players into categories is unnecessary and can do damage to their real relationships with players so I don't do it.

What you really need to know about your players is that they are people with all of the depth and complexity of real human beings. They think and they feel and they behave. Your job is to have strategies for understanding their thinking and helping to make it more effective where it is getting in the way of their performance and team relationships. Your job is to accept their feelings as products of their thinking. Their feelings will become more appropriate and positive as their thinking becomes more self-affirming and effective.

Sellers of psychological snake oil will offer you ways of identifying the personality types of players so that you can predict their behavior or understand it. It is not important to be able to say what a player will do. It is important to be able to say what a player has done. If you can be good at describing what was done (or said) you are part of the way toward being able to give useful feedback and toward predicting likely future behavior without benefit of intervention.

Understanding behavior is a little more complex. The word "understand" has several dictionary definitions. They range from "to grasp the meaning or reasonableness of" to "to be thoroughly familiar with the character and propensities of" and include "having thorough or technical acquaintance with or expertness in the practice of." It may also be used to mean "to accept as a fact or truth or regard as plausible without utter certainty." When it comes to understanding player behavior I think the first one is the one that most coaches will be thinking is important. You will certainly wonder where in the nine levels of Hades some of their behavior came from. A grasp of the meaning or way to see it as reasonable can save you from having to assume that you have a complete "wack job" on your team or payroll. You must, however, be prepared for the occasional character that seems to inhabit a parallel universe much of the time. I guess that is a type of personality but you won't find it in any of the numerous "tools" for classifying personality. There is no color and no box in a 2 by 2 matrix for "complete psycho." You just have to come to that conclusion on your own.

Your job is to provide boundaries for their behavior and to teach effectiveness on and off the field of play. Sometimes you teach by instruction and sometimes you teach by example and sometimes you teach by accident. All legal and moral methods are valid. The important part of the process is that you are engaged and interested in their behavior. You are aware of it and you pay attention to it and you care about it and you want to understand it origins and you will listen about it and you will end up sometimes "getting it." You will not tolerate it when it is unacceptable and you will provide consequences for it that are either positive or negative depending on its nature and effect on the team and the player. You will not delude yourself into thinking that you can reliably predict it without being engaged with the person.

Human behavior is only predictable when defined specifically within clear boundaries. For example, the behavior of drug addicted people is reliable with regard to seeking out and taking the drugs. Within a given amount of time it is fairly easy to predict that an addict will engage in this behavior. When it comes to the strategies that they will employ to pursue drug taking the variance begins to be much greater. There are an apparently infinite number of ways to lie, cheat steal and otherwise be a totally self-centered victim.

To make things even more complicated, your team changes from year-to-year or season-to-season. Your team is like life and Forrest Gump's box of chocolates, you never know for certain what you're going to get. The good news is that you can be sure to get human beings who are fundamentally very much like you and that is a good thing. They have the same potential for greatness as well as evil and can go either way depending on choices they make at critical moments in life. Be there in the right way at those moments and you may get to have a role in the development of a future leader of nations.

CHAPTER 6   TRUST ISSUES

It is arguable that social compatibility also implies a measure of trust. I would agree to the extent that people who share a value system and elements of a culture tend to have some common behavior patterns and rituals. These shared components of community life tend to produce a certain predictability regarding behavior and predictability makes people trustworthy in some ways. The depth of trust required for an athletic team will usually require more.

Scholars describe three stages in the development of trust. The 1st is to establish the basis on which people and their teammates are prepared to work together (the mission/identity of the team). The 2nd is to start to develop trust through a positive experience of working together that strengthens mutual understanding between team members. The 3rd stage generally comes out of an extended period of fruitful collaboration, when the people involved come genuinely to like each other and establish a personal bond. Their thinking suggests that the longer you can keep a team together under positive circumstances the more trust will develop.

In some teams the initial level of trust may be sufficient, but most situations demand something more. Being a member of an athletic team often means being willing to put the team above self in some way, situation or circumstance. Giving up the ball because another player has a higher percentage shot or making the crucial block instead of carrying the ball or staying focused to make that putt on behalf of the team score even though you have no chance of an individual victory are all examples of the kinds of behaviors that players must be trusted to bring.

The enormous pressure to excel as an individual can work against players' willingness to earn the trust of their fellows at that level. It is your job to make that sort of trustworthiness an integral part of your team culture through your setting and enforcement of standards and through being a model. Remember that trust is often an issue even when the word is not used. It can be found at the heart of many other apparent issues.

I hear a lot from coaches and players about the importance of "team chemistry" as a factor in success. When we ask what that is we get various answers that point to a felt need for the members of the team to like one another and enjoy one another's company. It appears that team members and coaches alike do not want to "hang" with people that they don't like. I have a suspicion that there is more going on here than social compatibility.

A key to understanding teamwork is the fact that true interdependence is what separates a team from a simple group. Members of a group may share a value system, an environment and many elements of a culture, but if they are not interdependent they are not a team in the way that we mean team. For some teams this distinction is easy to see. Basketball and football teams, for example, simply cannot compete without interdependent action. The success of each attempt to score or move toward the goal rests on the actions of more than one person playing a predictable part in running a play or creating an opportunity. The interdependence within golf and tennis teams is less visible with the obvious exception of tennis doubles play.

Interdependence strongly implies trust and you like people that you trust and vice versa. Hence the assertions that team chemistry is important. Team members react to a lack of trust by expressing a dislike for one another and complain about a lack of team chemistry. The root cause of team chemistry problems is found in trust issues and trust issues usually come from poor role definition, a lack of communication skills among members of the team and from coach failures. I will focus on the coach failures since this is a book about coaching.

Things to Watch Out For

Favoritism can kill the trust between the coach and players as well as among players. I touched on this subject in Chapter 6 in talking about fairness. Suffice it to say that favoritism can be a perception even when it is not a fact. It is crucial to manage in a way that prevents the perception as well as the fact, but don't expect miracles. If you get any indication that any of your players see favoritism as a problem you will have to address it head-on with those players.

The way I like to approach such a discussion is to begin by getting clear on the actual, observed behavior that led the player(s) to the conclusion that you favor anyone unfairly. Something like, "What have I done that makes you think that I have been unfair to you or that created this impression of favoritism?" Unless you get something that clearly makes you guilty such as routinely excusing a player from meeting one of the performance standards that you have set, you must continue to probe for the roots of the perception.

One player that I know had some of the worst time management skills I have ever seen coupled with some of the best athletic performance skills. Other players on the team wanted the coach to apply more punishment for tardiness and absence than they saw and did not want to excuse these things on the basis of superior contributions to team success. This was a tough one for the coach to work with. The truth is that it is hard to have or defend a time clock world when you are not paying for time. If you are paying for results, as is the case with exempt employees and athletes you will tend to be flexible with this sort of behavior. Your challenge may be to help the rest of the team to understand why you tolerate this apparent variance from a standard and why you want them to tolerate it as well. Performance makes a difference. It always makes a difference and it <u>should</u> make a difference. In this case the person was not lazy or showing callous disregard for the rules. It was a matter of poor personal management. The practice and workout time that was missed was made up and then some at other times and the coach accepted that along with the superior performance during competition.

If the problem is, for example, that you spend more time during practice giving attention to some player or to the seniors or to the freshmen or whatever, you must clarify what makes that a problem for the complaining player(s). "How is that a problem for you and others?" might be a good place to start. "Are you telling me that you want more instruction or guidance from me than I have given you?" might be another. The key is to NOT defend your behavior but to look for causes and solutions. In most cases you will neither own the problem nor be responsible for implementing the solution but you are in charge of the investigation and you do have a vested interest in the problem being solved.

An investigation, by the way, is an inquiry into the FACTS of a situation. You are responsible for the first level of investigation in all cases. You must be genuinely curious about what the players perceive and think and ask sincere questions that will help you to understand these things. Genuine investigation shows that you care and want to find a solution. It does not make you the owner of the problem or responsible for the solution - even though you may be.

You do not need to defend even when you are guilty. If you are not guilty and are only doing your job well then find out what the problem is for the player(s) so that you can help them to see things more realistically. A realistic view should put the player perceptions in perspective. First of all it is not any player's business that you choose to make an extra effort to get the best performance out of other players. You may give attention to a player because your educated eye sees talent that can be developed to help the team to a new level of performance. While there may be talent in every player some simply reek with possibilities for greatness. If the complaining player is asking for feedback or an assessment of potential then provide it and forget the favoritism issue. It was never the real problem.

A realistic view always includes an answer to the question of who owns the problem (mistake, misperception, misplacement of emotion or whatever) and who will be taking some action to solve the problem. That will almost always be the player(s). You may be able to help but you should never, never take ownership of something that is not yours.

If you discover that you are actually favoring some player(s) unfairly then you DO own the problem and must commit to changing what you are doing. Feedback is a gift when it informs you about how to do a better job. If you are not getting information that enables you to either help your players or points you in a better direction as a coach then it isn't feedback. It is a place to start. It is an indication that you have something to learn and perhaps a need for some good informative feedback.

Complaints about favoritism come from a variety of sources. They come from ignorance of the facts in a situation. They come from attempts to manipulate - which have their roots in feelings of powerlessness. They come from inappropriate expressions of feelings about other players (inappropriate if no effort has been put toward working through those feelings directly with the other player). They come from attempts to retaliate for hurt feelings. Sometimes they come from legitimate observations of behavior that you should change. You are not perfect, but you are a model. Good models demonstrate how to be wrong graciously and change what is useful to change. One of my clients changed the climate in her team dramatically by simply making it a habit to check in with each team member every day to overcome a perception of distance that diminished trust in her.

Reliable information is essential to performance and to trust. A wealth of studies has demonstrated that the "boss" is everyone's preferred source of information regarding what is going on with their work. That preference rapidly shifts to almost any other source that appears credible if the boss proves unreliable. A general rule that works is to communicate accurately, consistently and often.

Information includes anything that relates to team goals, the performance accountabilities of team members, what is expected of team members regarding things like attitude, what is going on with the powers that be outside the team (administration, boosters, media, etc.) and feedback on performance/behavior. There are always the three questions that frame the essential information that supports performance. Once again, they are, "What's my job?" "How am I doing?" and "Who cares?" Answer these every chance you get and every day if you can and you have gone way down the road to a sufficiently informed team.

One way to demonstrate the reliability of information is repetition. This is particularly true with regard to information about goals, accountabilities and expectations. Never forget that reliability implies trustworthiness. Good coaches and good managers alike will frequently refer to goals, standards and expectations when framing any discussion about the team. The more consistent their messages about these things the more trustworthy they appear.

The power of truth should never be underestimated when it comes to building trust. Children learn very quickly when adults are lying to them either by statement or omission of information. The less they see adults as a source of truth the more they will seek information from less valid sources. The same is true for you and your players. What you say has to respect the truth and how you say it has to respect sources, subjects and recipients.

You must remember, though that the power of truth can cut more than one way. It is not smart to tell everything you know that is true and feel justified because it is true. You have to be better than the run-of-the-mill humans at respecting confidences. Ask yourself if sharing some truth will add value in some way or simply make you look good, innocent or important. If it does not add value don't share it.

There are a few principles that you should remember:

1. **There are no such things as casual or private conversations.** Every interaction must be conducted with the same unshaken devotion to honesty and respect for others. Almost never tell a
player something in confidence because he or she is unlikely to respect that condition. There are conversations that should be conducted in private but don't make the mistake of thinking that what is said will not be leaked to others. The idea of "plausible deniability" did not come only from a desire to disinform or protect evildoers. It also came from the reality that the only way to be able to deny having said something is having no witnesses.

2. **Psychological trauma can have a long half life.** If you have a player with whom you have struggled and who perceives you to be responsible for some psychological pain do not expect that perception or that pain to go away quickly or easily. You should do all that you can to help heal the hurt, but that may not get you forgiven. Many people have a very hard time with forgiving. Some will justify their feelings with an old saw about forgiving but not forgetting. That is a distinction without a difference and means nothing except that forgiveness will not be forthcoming.

3. **Players sometimes hear what they most fear.** If a player fears criticism your best efforts to give informative, helpful feedback may be interpreted as critical judgment. You have no control over this sort of perceptual distortion. You just have to accept that it can happen and you will have to deal with it. Routinely checking for what the player heard during any conversation is important. It is especially important when you are discussion performance.

4. **People often "leak" more emotions than they deliberately project.** You will serve yourself well if you practice seeing emotions in others. Learn to play poker. Ask a loved one to tell you if guesses about their emotional states are right or wrong (do this only over dinner or during comfortable conversation and not

during disagreements). If you are introverted you will have to work especially hard at this because the research shows that you will have to focus more than will an extrovert in order to "see" emotions in others.

The role of the coach is variable as well depending upon the type of team. Football and basketball coaches are quite directly involved in the game during play. Golf and tennis coaches are much less directly involved in the game but play a critical role nonetheless.

CHAPTER 7   CAN I SMACK 'EM NOW?

Generally the answer is no. We have not found any situations in which physical violence has proven to be successful in changing behavior. That does not mean that it is not a sometimes attractive option. Childlike behavior coming from people who should be more adult is incredibly frustrating. It is made even more so by the protests of those same people that they should be treated like adults. It is hard to have empathy and positive regard for people who whine and complain when it is clear that more effective strategies would involve seeking and accepting adult accountability. Victim behavior encourages those of us who take perverse pleasure in persecution to ply our trade. The net outcome of any kind of violent action, however, is ugly and undesirable despite the momentary pleasure associated with ripping out the heart of someone who so richly deserves it.

Okay, I was just kidding about the actual heart ripping. The truth is that few coaches actually resort to that, Bobby Knight's behavior notwithstanding. What normally happens is that the violence takes a different form. It comes out in angry outbursts and other cruel and demeaning behaviors.

Yelling at players is probably the most visible form of violence that coaches choose, but it is probably not the most common. Another is sarcasm Personally, I like to think of sarcasm as an intellectual art form. It involves an artful turn of phrase and an understanding of satire and irony. Among friends it can earn respect up to a point. Between coaches and players it is a weapon designed to inflict pain. And it works to a fare thee well. Avoid it.

The Worst Case

Sometimes the damage that has been done to relationships is beyond recovery. People are rarely able to get over past hurts and move on. There are many possible reasons for this apparent intransigence, but the reasons don't really matter. The kinds of changes that are necessary often include changes to personnel as well as changes to systems, processes and behavior.

I always advise a large dose of patience with even the worst cases. You may be one small event or conversation away from that teachable moment that will allow you to help a player to turn around, but you have to weigh that against current reality. If a player is not simply under-performing but is doing damage to team cohesion you may have to take administrative action. Releasing a player is a very serious step for both the player and the coach. Many times the administration will get involved as well. There are similar situations in the business world where the decision to terminate a person for any but the most serious of infractions takes time and input from several layers of management and several staff functions like HR and the Legal Dept. When it must be done it must be done quickly and with sensitivity.

This is a short chapter because it is not where your head should be. I almost avoided it altogether but that would have been dishonest.

CHAPTER 8   AFTER ALL IS SAID AND DONE

It is usually true that after all is said and done there is much more said than done. That's okay in the real world. There should be more time and effort put into planning than into rework anyway so lots of dialogue about what should happen in the future is a good thing. Lots of dialogue about what should have happened in the past is a complete waste of time. If there is good information about mistakes that were made and contingencies that were not foreseen, then use that information for planning not for recriminations.

I began this little guidebook with some thoughts about coaching as an honorable profession. I remain convinced that it is. Coaching has tremendous potential for touching the lives of people both young and old. Touching lives is a sacred trust and any person whose occupation calls for it must understand the heavy burden of responsibility that is taken on with the job. In the end you may find that the real work of coaching, which has less to do with the game and more to do with the infrastructure that enables the game, is not so desirable and not what you signed up for. If that is the case please walk away from it. There are too many lives involved for a person to stay in this role without loving it.

The fundamental truth is that you do not coach a sport you coach people. That means that this whole thing is not about you. It is about them. Your work as a coach has to be "them-centered" in order for it to have the quality necessary for great performance.

I know that you have feelings and that you want your players to care about you and to want your guidance and instruction. You want them to look up to you and to remember you as an important person in their lives. I know you want all of this and if you do the job well you will get enough of it. You cannot, however, build your coaching around meeting these needs of yours. They are by-products of doing the job well and not central goals.

It is about them. It is about their goals and their skills and their needs and their growth and their petty nonsense upon which you must focus and that you must develop and which you must understand and that you must foster and which you must tolerate. That is a really bad sentence but I don't know how to say it another way. The players get to make a lot more mistakes than you do. The reality may be that we are all learning every day as long as we live but the things that you are learning should have more to do with fine tuning your skills and achieving deeper understanding of yourself. The players are learning real basic fundamentals about their game and about living in the world.

It is about them and your mission is their performance. Accolades as a coach are not what you work for. You work for great performance from great kids that you choose who grow and blossom in the environment you create. Accolades will come if you do that stuff really well and good fortune smiles upon you. Life ain't fair so it is possible that you can do everything really well and still get no respect or recognition. So it goes in the real world. So what? Grown up mature people do the job anyway out of love for the sport and for the kids and for the opportunity to produce excellence.

I have the same message for anyone who would become a supervisor or manager and the higher the level of management to which the person aspires the more loudly I exclaim, "Do this only if you can do ALL of the job!!!" "All of the job" means dealing every day with the three key questions (What's my job? How am I doing?

Who cares?). It means being hard-nosed about the bottom line and deeply caring about the people whose lives you touch.

The decision to be a coach should not be taken lightly. Any job that puts you in a position to influence the quality of life of others is a sacred trust. Treat it as such and you will reap rewards of the greatest magnitude. And you will never, as we used to say when I was in the US military, "have to back up to the pay window" (because you could not face the paymaster when you had not really done the job). You will hold your head high and sleep comfortably (except for during championship play) and you will have the deep and lasting joy of knowing that you did the right things when nobody was looking. You will know that you did the right things for those kids that you would really rather have smacked at time. You will know that you added value in the world in the ways that only a parent, coach or manager can for the power in those roles is awesome.

So if you decide to become or continue to be a COACH or MANAGER of people, hitch up your socks and go for it. You are choosing a role with nearly unparalleled influence on the quality of human life. You will have a better chance of being one of the good guys than most.

You should end up being proud of your accomplishments but please don't fall into the trap of measuring them only in terms of a won-lost record. Certainly that is important but you will be engaged in another competition of perhaps greater importance. That is the fight to deliver good people into the world at large. For parents, teachers, coaches and bosses of all kinds this is your greatest contribution. It's what a 9, 9 Coach does.